itty-bitty nursery

itty-bitty nursery

Susan B. Anderson

Photographs by Liz Banfield

ARTISAN
NEW YORK

ALSO BY SUSAN B. ANDERSON

itty-bitty hats

Published by Artisan

A Division of Workman Publishing Company, Inc.

225 Varick Street

New York, NY 10014-4381

www.artisanbooks.com

Library of Congress Cataloging-in-Publication Data

Anderson, Susan B.

itty-bitty nursery / Susan B. Anderson.

p. cm

ISBN-13: 978-1-57965-334-7

1. Knitting—Patterns. 2. Infants' supplies. I. Title.

TT825.A55 2007

746.43'2041—dc22

2006047938

Design by Jan Derevjanik
and Stephanie Huntwork

Printed in Malaysia

First printing, September 2007

2 4 6 8 10 9 7 5 3 1

To my husband, Brian, and children,

Evan, Ben, Holly, and Mary Kate.

You make my house a home.

And to my mom, Mary Ann Barrett.

Thank you for a lifetime filled with love and support.

contents

introduction

When I shared a copy of *Itty-Bitty Hats*, my first book, with a dear friend of mine, she turned to me and said, "You have a voice!" I loved that reaction, and this comment has resonated in my thoughts for a long time. I know that I have always had a strong voice when it came to my own knitting, but I began thinking about every knitter's voice. Each knitter has a distinct perspective about his or her knitting. Knitters share their viewpoints with others through the choices they make when working on a project.

These choices are initially fairly basic: which projects to make and which yarns to use. Adding a personal twist to a pattern through color choice or other variation can make a project different from anyone else's. Even if you don't make any changes to a pattern, no two handknitted items are the same. I thus want to encourage knitters to jump into *Itty-Bitty Nursery* with abandon. Don't hesitate to make these patterns your own through your choices. This wonderful act of baby knitting is an expression of your knitting voice. There is no better way to send a message of love to a baby.

I have dreamt about a fantastic knitted nursery forever, and so I let my imagination and needles run wild for this collection. Making lists of every baby-loving item I could think of, I then knitted them like a tornado until I had enough projects, and even some extras. The promise of *Itty-Bitty Nursery* is that you can knit up an entire nursery with clothes, toys, room adornments, blankets, pillows, and baby accessories, the type of nursery where we want every baby to live and grow. Now, even I know that not everyone has time to knit every project offered here, but this is where your own knitting voice comes into play. Pick the projects that speak to you, the ones you *ooh* and *aah* over, or simply the goodies you are just itching to start. These are the gifts that will best express your joy and love for the new baby in your life.

In this collection I have offered a variety of projects for every level of knitter, including the most inexperienced. There is a chapter that uses only garter stitch squares, the most basic starting point, to complete a wide variety of projects that are truly beautiful. For all levels of knitters there are toys for any age child (as well as adults), lovely blankets, a pure-white layette set, whimsical pillows that could be used anywhere in the house, a felted bag for Mom, and so much more. Even my older children are excited about many of these projects. When selecting the recipient of your next project from *Itty-Bitty Nursery*, keep all ages in mind. Many of these designs are not just for babies!

But, of course, all babies deserve a knitted nursery of their own, even if it contains only one or two knitted items. Knitting is an act of pure love, and who better to shower this love on than a baby?

Peace, love, and knit for beautiful babies everywhere!

abbreviations

k	knit
k2tog	knit two stitches together as one stitch
ssk	slip two stitches separately as if to knit, knit these two stitches together through the back loops
p	purl
p2tog	purl two stitches together as one stitch
kfb	knit into the front loop and then into the back loop of the same stitch
pfb	purl into the front loop and then into the back loop of the same stitch
m1	make one stitch by inserting the left needle from the front to the back under the bar in between the right-most stitch on the left needle and the leftmost stitch on the right needle, making a loop on the left needle; knit the bar through the back loop
rs	right side
sl1	slip one stitch as if to purl
yo	yarn over

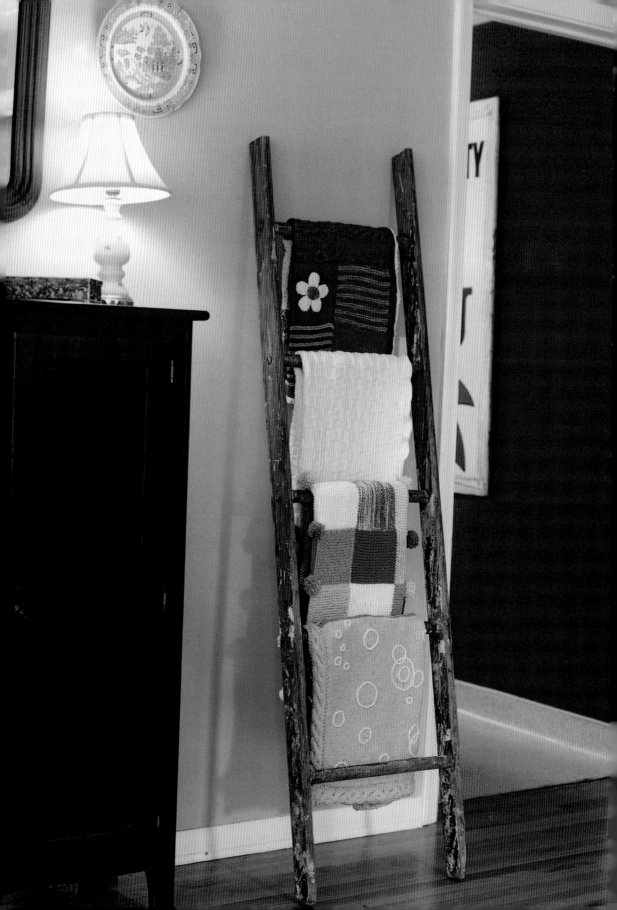

itty-bitty nursery

squares and rectangles

This entire chapter contains beautiful, one-of-a-kind projects made solely out of garter stitch squares and rectangles. Beginners, get ready for some serious fun. Experienced knitters, get ready for a few slick, easy projects to add to your gift repertoire! You might think that projects of this sort aren't going to be shapely or sophisticated, but just take a look. The lavender sweater, hat, and bootie set, for example, has a lovely elegance created with a decorative whipstitch and some silk ribbon ties. The door hanger/sachet has an embroidered detail and is filled with lavender seeds for a soothing scent.

The patchwork blanket is a snap to knit on your own or with a group of friends. The pom-pom edging adds just the right touch of fun to this comfy blanket. Of course, there has to be a friendly bear who's just the right size to tag along wherever your baby goes. The bear even has a matching sweater.

No matter which project you select, any level of knitter can quickly and simply create these sweet, elegant, and fun projects in no time at all. I've included an instructional section at the beginning of this chapter that includes the necessary skills to complete these projects. If you are a beginner, start here, and you'll find out that the secret to knitting is just a little determination. Once you give your first handknit gift, you will race back to your needles to begin the next one!

basic skills

The following skills are all you will need to complete these projects out of garter stich squares and rectangles. When you master them, you will be well on your way to becoming an accomplished knitter. More advanced techniques, which you will need to complete other projects later in *Itty-Bitty Nursery,* can be found in Special Techniques, starting on page 143.

CASTING ON

slipknot • The slipknot is the very first step in casting on to begin your project.

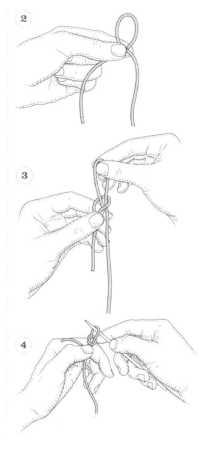

1. Measure out the length of yarn needed for the long-tail cast-on (which you'll learn below). The pattern you are about to begin will tell you how many stitches you will need to cast on. You can figure out how long the tail of the yarn needs to be by wrapping the yarn around the needle once for every stitch called for. Then add about another 8 inches. At this point in the yarn, you will make a slipknot.

2. Make a loop, overlapping the yarn at the bottom of the loop.

3. Bring the yarn that is to the front of the overlap behind and then through the loop, making another loop. Pull up.

4. Put the new loop on the needle and tighten it to fit.

   TIP • Always include the slipknot when counting stitches!

long-tail cast-on • I use this method of casting on for almost every project I start. I think it looks clean, and it gives the right amount of stretch to my work.

1. With the slipknot on the needle, hold the needle with your right hand and let the yarn hang down. The yarn attached to the ball (the working yarn) should be behind the needle, and the yarn tail should be toward you.

2. Pinch the index finger and thumb of your left hand together and stick them between the strands of yarn hanging from the needle.

3. Open up your left index finger and thumb to form a V. The tail end of the yarn will be over your left thumb, and the working yarn will be over your index finger. Turn your hand so your palm is facing you, and hold both strands of yarn against your palm with the other fingers of your left hand.

4. Bring the right needle point around the outside of the yarn on your thumb, then under the yarn. Then bring your needle up through the loop around your thumb, over, and around the outside of and under the yarn on your index finger. Turn the needle downward and pull it back through the loop around your thumb. Gently slip the yarn from around your thumb.

5. Without dropping the yarn held on your palm, put your thumb back under the tail end of the yarn and pull the stitch up firmly, but be sure the stitch can slide a bit on the needle.

• Repeat steps 4 and 5 until you have the required number of stitches on your needle. Remember to count your slipknot as one stitch.

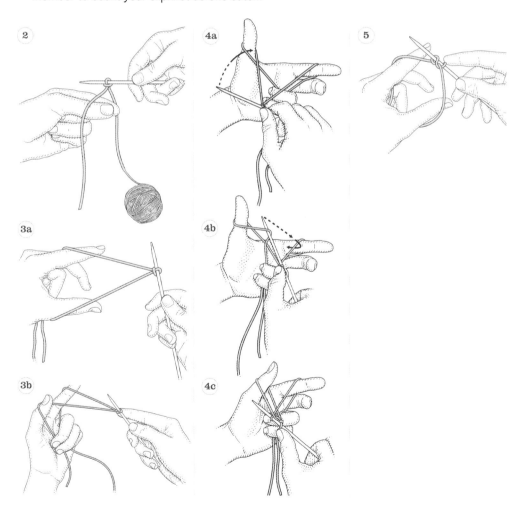

This is the continental style of knitting. It is fine to use other styles of knitting since you get the same result with all of these.

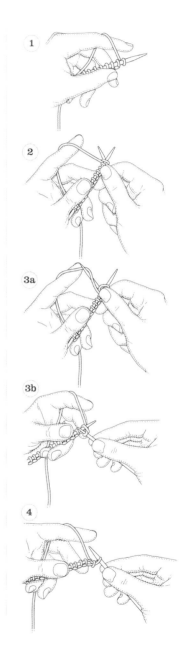

1. Hold the needle with the cast-on stitches in your left hand with the yarn over your left index finger.

2. With your right hand, place the point of the right needle into the first loop on the left needle, inserting the needle point from bottom to top and from front to back (behind the left needle). The points of the needles will form an X. Hold the X together with your right hand, with your thumb in front and your index finger in back.

3. Wrap the yarn that is on your index finger counter-clockwise around the point of the right needle. After wrapping, the yarn should end up at the back of the right needle. Tip the point of the right needle down-ward and pull the loop through the stitch, keeping the loop on the right needle.

4. Slip the completed stitch off the left needle. Be sure not to pull any other stitches off with it. The new stitch is now on the right needle.

• Here is a chant for you to say to yourself as you knit the four steps of the knit stitch:
   In (2),
   Around (3a),
   Out (3b),
   Off (4).

> TIP • I squeeze the yarn between my index finger and middle finger at the knuckle in order to create tension, but others additionally wrap the yarn around their ring finger or little finger or find other ways to make the yarn taut. Experiment to discover what works best for you.

basic bind-off • When you get to the end of a project or piece and you want to remove it from the needles, you use a technique called binding off. It is far simpler than casting on, and new knitters are pleasantly surprised at how easy this step is. One problem to be aware of is binding off too tightly. This becomes a problem on projects such as sweaters, where necklines can be bound off so tightly that the sweater will literally not fit over the head of the wearer. There is an easy remedy for this. Simply bind off using a needle that is two sizes larger than the needle you are currently using. Hold this larger needle in your right hand and work the stitches onto this needle. If you don't use a larger needle, just make sure you are making a conscious effort to bind off loosely by knitting each stitch of the bind-off row loosely.

1. Knit 2 stitches onto the right needle.

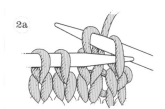

2. Using the tip of your left needle, pass the right stitch on the right needle over the left stitch and off the needle. (I used to use my fingers to pick up the stitch and pass it over when I first started knitting.)

3. Knit the next stitch onto the right needle and repeat step 2.

• Repeat steps 2 and 3 until you have the desired number of bound-off stitches. You'll have 1 stitch remaining on your right needle. If you are at the end of a project or piece, cut your yarn, leaving a tail. Pull the tail through the last stitch and pull it up tight.

GARTER STITCH

All of the projects in this section are knit in garter stitch, which simply means that you knit every stitch of each row. This is the easiest, most basic stitch in knitting because you only have to know how to complete the knit stitch; there is no purling involved. Garter stitch creates a sturdy fabric that has ridges and lays flat at the edges.

GAUGE

Gauge is always important, but it is even more important when you are hoping to make a great-fitting garment. When you are making a toy or blanket, if your gauge is a tiny bit off it won't ruin the finished project. The gauge throughout this book refers to the number of stitches per inch across each row, and sometimes the number of rows per inch as well. Both of these numbers determine the width and length of your knitted piece. This number varies depending on the yarn and the needle size you are using, as well as your personal knitting tension—how loosely or tightly you knit. For the latter reason especially, it is important to always make a gauge swatch before starting your project. Always try to use the yarn that is recommended, but if you have to substitute another yarn, it is very important to make a swatch. Make one as follows:

1. With your selected yarn and needles, cast on 20 stitches.

2. Knit in pattern stitch for 4 inches.

3. Slip the knitted fabric off the needle without casting off.

4. Lay the swatch flat on a table and let the yarn take its natural shape. Do not tug or stretch the fabric, unless instructed to in the pattern.

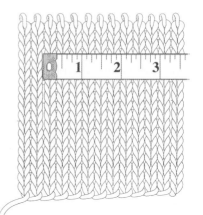

5. Set your ruler on top of the knitting with the right side of the fabric facing you. In garter stitch, both sides of the work will be made up of ridges and valleys. In stockinette stitch, the right side is made up of small Vs.

6. Choosing a section near the center of the swatch, count how many stitches there are in 1 inch, including half and quarter stitches.

> TIP • Many times, when a project is small, you can begin it as directed in the pattern, knowing that after you have knitted a couple of inches, you can check your gauge.

KEY INFORMATION FOR GAUGE AND NEEDLE SIZE

- If the number of stitches in 1 inch of your swatch matches the required number of stitches per inch in the pattern, then you are ready to start.

- If there are too many stitches per inch, use larger needles.

- If there are too few stitches per inch, use smaller needles.

- If you need to change needle size, move up or down by one size. Keep making new swatches until you obtain the correct gauge.

FINISHING OR SEAMING

Sewing garter stitch edges together is simple and, best of all—due to the bumpy nature of the fabric—it is forgiving. This basic seaming technique is perfect for sewing together squares or the sides of a bear.

garter stitch seam

With the edges you wish to join lined up next to each other and right sides facing you, cut a length of yarn and thread it into a yarn needle so you are working with a single thickness of yarn. Do not knot the end of the yarn. Starting at the left edge, insert the needle into the top loop (a purl stitch bump) and draw the yarn through the loop nearly to the end. Leave a 3-inch tail. On the corresponding stitch on the right edge, insert the needle into the bottom loop (a knit stitch). Do not draw the stitches up too tightly—try to match the tightness of the knitting, but do not leave gaps in the seam. Continue alternating the sides with a top loop and a bottom loop. When the seam is completed, weave in both ends of the seaming yarn and trim close to the knitted piece.

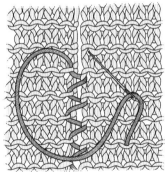

GARTER STITCH SEAM

Insert the yarn needle into the top bump on one side, then the bottom bump of the corresponding stitch on the other side. Continue to alternate in this way.

whipstitch seam

With the edges you wish to join lined up next to each other and right sides facing you, cut a length of yarn and thread it into a yarn needle. Starting on the right side, insert the needle into the stitch at the edge. On the corresponding stitch on the left edge, insert the needle. Gently pull the yarn through, keeping an even tension. The whipstitch seam can be used on any type of knitted piece.

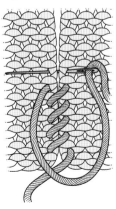

WHIPSTITCH SEAM

Decorative whipstitch is used on the Squares and Rectangles Baby Set to seam the pieces and create textural interest. The edges are held together with the right sides facing out, and the needle is inserted through both layers at the same time. Although the whipstitch stitches for this sweater set are placed very close together, the stitch can also be spaced farther apart.

1. Line up the edges of the pieces with either the right sides together or the wrong sides together. The pattern will tell you which is required. You can pin the pieces together if you need to.

2. Thread a tail end or new piece of yarn into a yarn needle. Holding the edges together, insert the needle 1 stitch in from the edge, from back to front, going through both pieces at the same time.

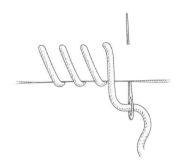

3. Pull the yarn through. Bring the needle around to the back side and insert it again in the next stitch.

* Repeat steps 2 and 3 as needed, then weave in the yarn ends.

squares and rectangles
baby set

Sometimes things just have to be easy, and these projects are exactly that. If you can knit a garter stitch square, you can make this adorable, stylish baby cardigan, hat, booties, and sachet set. Another option is to assign the squares and rectangles to different friends to work together for a fantastic group baby gift. Then simply whipstitch and sew up the seams and you have the most thoughtful gifts for a new baby and mom.

For a more boyish option for the cardigan, hat, and booties, you could make the front exactly the same as the back, creating a boatneck sweater rather than a cardigan. Leave out the ribbon and make two pom-poms for the corners of the hat, and two for the tops of the booties. Follow the rest of the pattern as is, and you have instant boy!

The ribbon is attached to all of the pieces with a simple single knot. This makes for easy removal of the ribbon before washing the garments.

yarn

- RY Classic Yarns Cashsoft Baby DK (57% extra fine merino, 33% microfiber, 10% cashmere; 142 yards/
50 grams), Borage #806. Cardigan: 3 skeins; Hat: 1 skein; Booties: 1 skein

tools

- U.S. size 7 needles or size needed to obtain gauge

- 2½-inch-wide silk ribbon. See individual projects for required lengths.

- Straight or safety pins
- Scissors
- Yarn needle
- Ruler or tape measure

sizes for the cardigan, hat, and booties

- 0–3 months (3–6 months, 6–12 months)

gauge for all pieces (except sachet)

- 5 stitches per inch

NOTE • The yarn is the same for the cardigan, hat, and booties; the amounts vary and are specified. The tools, sizes, and gauge are the same throughout. The same ribbon is used for all the projects, and the lengths required for each are specified. The sachet requires different yarn colors gauge, and tools, which are specified at the beginning of the pattern.

cardigan

ribbon

- 4 feet of 2½-inch-wide silk ribbon

BACK

Cast on 45 (48, 50) stitches. Work in garter stitch until the back measures 9 (9½, 10) inches. Bind off all stitches.

FRONT

The front is made in four pieces: two squares and two rectangles.

bottom fronts (make 2) • Cast on 22 (24, 25) stitches. Work in garter stitch until the piece measures 5 (5½, 6) inches. Bind off all stitches.

top fronts (make 2) • Cast on 22 (24, 25) stitches. Work in garter stitch until the piece measures 4 inches. Bind off all stitches.

sleeves (make 2) • Cast on 30 (35, 38) stitches. Work in garter stitch until the sleeve measures 5 (5½, 6) inches. Bind off all stitches.

FINISHING

Use a decorative whipstitch to sew the top and bottom fronts together. Hold the two pieces flat on top of each other, with the edges that measure 4½ (4¾, 5) inches aligned and wrong sides facing. (Determine garter stitch wrong side by looking at the cast-on row.) With a single thickness of yarn threaded into a yarn needle, whipstitch entire edge ¼ inch from the edge, placing the stitches close together to create a cordlike look. Weave in yarn ends and trim.

Use this same technique on the shoulder seams, starting at the outer edge and sewing the seams closed for 2 (2, 2½) inches.

Sew the sleeves on at the shoulders with a decorate whipstitch.

Seam the sleeves and the sides of the cardigans, using the garter seaming stitch detailed on page 9.

Use the decorative whipstitch around all of the edges of the cardigan. Begin at the front opening. Here I made the shape a little more interesting by stretching the fabric as I did the whipstitch, which creates points at the bottom front and top front. Leave the bottom points as they are, but take the top points of the fronts and stitch them down to the front to create a collarlike appearance.

Complete the neck opening, the bottom edge of the cardigan, and the cuffs of the sleeves with the decorative whipstitch.

ribbon tie • Cut two 24-inch pieces of the ribbon and thread one through each cardigan front right above the empire seam and about an inch in from the edge. Tie a single knot to secure. Trim the ends at an angle for a more finished look.

BACK

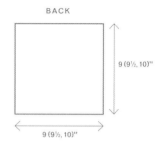

9 (9½, 10)"

9 (9½, 10)"

FRONTS

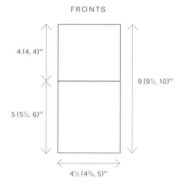

4 (4, 4)"

9 (9½, 10)"

5 (5½, 6)"

4½ (4¾, 5)"

SLEEVES

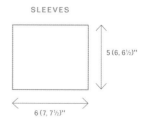

5 (6, 6½)"

6 (7, 7½)"

hat

ribbon

* 4 feet of 2½-inch-wide silk ribbon

HAT

Cast on 28 (32, 36) stitches. Work in garter stitch for 12 (13, 14) inches. Bind off all stitches.

FINISHING

Fold the rectangle in half, wrong sides together, aligning the cast-on edge and the bound-off edge. Pin the side seams of the hat together, then turn up 1 inch of the brim edge and pin into place. This forms the brim of the hat. Sew the sides together with the same decorative whipstitch described for the cardigan. Whipstitch over the turned-up brim of the hat to hold it in place. The seam should look like a cord. Whipstitch across the top of the hat to create a whipstich cord along the folded edge. Remove all pins.

ribbon ties • Cut two 24-inch pieces of ribbon. Pull one piece through each upper corner of the hat and tie in a bow. Trim the ribbon ends at an angle.

booties

These booties are made from one square for each foot.

ribbon

* 4 feet of 2½-inch-wide silk ribbon

FOOT (make 2)

Cast on 18 (20, 22) stitches. Work in garter stitch for 3½ (4, 5) inches. Do not cast off. Cut the working yarn, leaving an 18-inch tail, and thread into a yarn needle. Pull the yarn through the stitches on the knitting needle, remove the knitting needle from the work, and pull up tight to form the toe. Fold the rest of the square in half lengthwise and stitch, using the decorative whipstitch until the seam measures 1½ (2, 3) inches from the toe. Weave in the ends and trim.

FINISHING

Next sew the back of the foot using a garter stitch seam (see p. 9).

ribbon ties • Cut two 24-inch pieces of ribbon. Thread the end into a yarn needle. Thread yarn through garter stitch bumps around the edge of the foot opening. Pull the ribbon through until the ends are even. Tie in a bow.

hanging sachet

This lovely multipurpose project could be used as a door hanger to mark the nursery, a wall hanging over the changing table, or, without the ribbon, a sachet for baby's drawer. If you changed the embroidery to mère, which is French for "mother," it would make a perfect mother's sachet. Why not make a matching pair for mom and baby both! I used sweet, soothing lavender to fill the sachet, but you could use your own favorite scent.

yarn

- RY Classic Yarns Cashsoft Baby DK (57% extra fine merino, 33% microfiber, 10% cashmere; 142 yards/50 grams), 1 skein in Snowman #800, small amount of Borage #806 for embroidery

tools

- U.S. size 4 needles or size needed to obtain gauge
- U.S. size G crochet hook
- 52 inches of 2½-inch-wide silk ribbon
- ½ cup of lavender seeds
- Small bag of polyester fiberfill
- Scissors
- Yarn needle

finished measurement

- 5½ inches by 4½ inches

gauge

- 6 stitches per inch

RECTANGLE (make 2)

Cast on 34 stitches. Work in garter stitch for 4½ inches. Bind off all stitches.

EMBROIDERY

With Borage and the crochet hook, chain stitch on the surface of the pieces, spelling out bébé (see p. 154). Leave a 1-inch space unstitched around the edge. Cut a long length of Borage and thread into a yarn needle. Tightly wrap the chained letters as detailed on page 159. Weave in the ends on the wrong side.

FINISHING

Place the two pieces on top of each other, wrong sides together, with the bébé side facing you. With a length of Snowman and a yarn needle, backstitch three sides together about ¼ inch from the edge. Turn the bébé side face down on the table. Pour the ½ cup of lavender inside so it covers the bébé side. Fill the rest of the sachet with the fiberfill stuffing, laying it over the top of the lavender so it is a little puffy but not overstuffed. Close the fourth side using the backstitch, ¼ inch from the edge. Weave in ends and trim.

ribbon ties • Cut two 26-inch pieces of ribbon. Tie one on each top corner of the sachet with a single knot. Tie the two long ends together and make a bow.

grumpy old bear

After I made this bear, my kids all told me at separate times that he looked grumpy. Really? I didn't mean for this bear to be grumpy! Then my sister laughed when she saw the bear and said he is so cute and grumpy. I thought about changing the face, but decided maybe he is just meant to be that way, and I don't want to mess with fate. I love this grumpy old bear no matter what.

What's amazing about this sweet bear is that you'd never know it's made completely out of garter stitch squares. This means that *anyone* can knit this bear. Seaming garter stitch is very forgiving. Don't worry about perfect seams if you are a beginner. This will be great practice.

yarn

- **Rowan Handknit Cotton (100% cotton; 93 yards/50 grams), 2 skeins in Linen #205**

tools

- **U.S. size 3 needles or size needed to obtain gauge**
- **One skein of black embroidery floss**
- **Small bag of polyester fiberfill**
- **Small bag of poly-pellets**
- **Scissors**
- **Yarn needle**
- **Ruler or tape measure**

gauge

- **6 stitches per inch**

finished size

- **8 inches tall**

BODY AND HEAD

Cast on 36 stitches. Work in garter stitch until piece measures 5½ inches. Do not bind off. Cut the working yarn, leaving an 8-inch tail. Thread the tail into a yarn needle and pull through the live stitches on the knitting needle. Remove knitting needle from piece. Pull up the yarn and gather the work at the top as tightly as possible. There may still be a slight hole, so take a few stitches with the needle to close up any gap.

This will be the bottom of the bear's body. Starting at the bottom, sew the side seam, using a garter stitch seam. Stuff the bear by filling it half full of the poly-pellets and the rest of the way with the fiberfill until the bear is firm.

EARS

When you have sewn the side seam and reach the top corner, pinch the corner and wrap the yarn a few times: around this pinched section to create an ear. Stitch once to secure. Continue sewing across the top of the head and pinch, gather, and stitch the other corner to create the other ear. Weave in end and trim.

NECK

Measure 2 inches down from the top of the head; this is where the neck will be. With a length of yarn on a yarn needle, use the running stitch to encircle the bear at that point. When you have stitched all the way around, pull the yarn very tightly to cinch in the neck. Take a few stitches to hold the gathers in place and weave in the ends to the inside.

NOSE

Cast on 7 stitches. Work in garter stitch for 1 inch. Bind off. Cut yarn, leaving a 6-inch end, and thread the tail into a yarn needle. Fold the corners of the square toward the square's center to form the piece into a flat circle. Place a tiny amount of fiberfill in the center of the nose and sew the nose onto the face.

Using the photograph as a guide, with the black embroidery floss and a yarn needle, take 2 stitches for each eye. Use satin stitch (see p. 157) to create the nose and mouth.

ARMS (make 2)

Cast on 16 stitches. Work in garter stitch for 2½ inches. Cut the yarn and leave an 8-inch tail. Thread tail into a yarn needle and draw needle through all stitches. Remove knitting needle from work and gather stitches tightly to form the end of the arm. Sew the side seam of the arm and stuff with fiberfill until firm. Sew across the top to create the shoulder. One inch up from the gathered end, use the running stitch to gather the arm and create a hand.

Repeat.

When you have two arms ready to sew onto the bear, line them up on either side of the bear close to the neck gathering. Attach the arms by pushing the yarn needle and yarn through one arm at the shoulder, going all the way through to the other arm, and then going back through again. Pull tight, and take a few stitches to keep the arms in place. Weave in the ends to the inside.

LEGS (make 2)

Cast on 16 stitches. Work in garter stitch for 2 inches. Cut the yarn, leaving a 6-inch end and thread into a yarn needle. Pull needle through the live stitches and gather up tightly. Sew up the seam and stuff the leg with fiberfill until firm. Sew across the cast-on edge. Sew the cast-on edge to the bottom of the bear body, placing the legs more toward the front of the body. This allows the bear to sit better.

FEET (make 2 of each part)

top of feet • Cast on 8 stitches. Work in garter stitch for 1 inch. Bind off all stitches.

bottom of feet • Cast on 12 stitches. Work in garter stitch for 1½ inches. Bind off all stitches. Place the top of one foot on top of one bottom, lining up the cast-on and bound-off edges. Sew around three of the edges, with a whipstitch, folding the bottom in to fit the top piece. Fill the foot with the poly-pellets until firm. Sew the fourth edge together. Sew the foot to the gathered end of the leg, attaching it at the top of the foot. Repeat for the second foot.

SCARF

yarn

- Any DK or worsted-weight yarn (small amount needed)

NOTE • The sample is made in Koigu Kersti.

tools

- U.S. size 7 needles
- U.S. size G crochet hook
- Scissors
- Ruler or tape measure

With size 7 needles, cast on 5 stitches. Work in garter stitch for 11 inches. Bind off all stitches.

Make fringe by cutting sixteen 2-inch strands (see p. 153). Hold two pieces together and make four fringes for each end of the scarf. Trim the fringe so it is even.

bear sweater

This sweater fits the Grumpy Old Bear like a glove! Use your leftover yarn and ribbon from the Squares and Rectangles Baby Set to outfit him in an adorable garment constructed completely out of garter stitch squares and rectangles. The main ideas here are easy, easy, and easy!

yarn

- RY Classic Yarns Cashsoft Baby DK (57% extra fine merino, 33% microfiber, 10% cashmere); 1 skein or the leftover yarn from the Squares and Rectangles Baby Set in Borage #806

tools

- U.S. size 7 needles or size needed to obtain gauge
- 18 inches of 2½-inch-wide silk ribbon
- Scissors
- Yarn needle
- Ruler or tape measure

gauge

- 5 stitches per inch

BACK

Cast on 22 stitches. Work in garter stitch until piece measures 3 inches. Bind off.

FRONT (make 2)

Cast on 11 stitches. Work in garter stitch until piece measures 3 inches. Bind off.

SLEEVES (make 2)

Cast on 14 stitches. Work in garter stitch until piece measures 1 inch. Bind off.

FINISHING

Using a whipstitch seam throughout, sew shoulders together for 1 inch in from the shoulder edge. Sew sleeves onto the sweater body. Sew side seams. Fold down the front top corners and stitch to create a collar. Cut the ribbon into two 9-inch pieces. Thread each piece into a yarn needle, and pull through each sweater front and tie one end in a single-knot on the outside of the sweater. Cut the ends at an angle, and tie together in a bow.

patches

This patchwork blanket has loads of possibilities. It can be a fantastic project for you to knit alone or an excellent group knitting project. Either way, it is as easy as pie! I purposely made the squares relatively small with the group project in mind, so at least one square could be contributed by anyone, even a brand-new knitter. Asking a beginner to knit an entire large panel or even a large square may mean it may not get done in time or even at all, disappointing the rest of the knitters.

One easy way to divide this project up is to gather seven friends willing to participate. There are forty-nine squares total, so each of these friends will knit seven squares, which requires two skeins of yarn. The leftover yarn is used for the pom-poms that are attached around the border. If the newbie knitters can't manage seven squares each, just spread the knitting duties around so everyone feels comfortable. Even if the new knitters contribute one square each or someone is in charge just of making the pom-poms, that is exactly what makes this type of project the most endearing gift for a new baby.

Seaming the squares together is a snap using the whipstitch seaming technique described on page 9. The only trick is to be consistent. You could divide the blanket into sections for seaming by different people, or you could get together and do it all at once. I like to lay the squares out on large table or floor and start playing with the layout of the colors. I like the randomness of not having a distinct pattern in this type of blanket. Be creative and make up your own layout.

> TIP • You want to try to achieve a similar gauge for all of the squares, even if different people are knitting, but I have sewn many blankets together where the gauges are all over the place. The end results have been extremely charming anyway. So pay some attention to gauge, but don't get crazy about it. There are ways to fudge a bit when sewing up the seams, knitted fabric is very flexible, and you can do a lot with blocking (see p. 150), too.

yarn

Sample Version (blues, grays, and white)

* GGH Samoa (50% cotton, 50% microfiber; 104 yards/50 grams), 2 skeins each in White #18, Light Blue #85, Pale Blue #91, Denim Blue #56, Light Gray #69, and Gray #27; Rowan All Seasons Cotton (60% cotton, 40% microfiber; 98 yards/50 grams), 2 skeins in Glad #208

Alternate Version (pinks, white, and yellow)

* GGH Samoa, 2 skeins each of White #18, Bright Pink #37, Light Pink #52, Rose #89, Butter Yellow #93, and Dark Pink #99; Rowan All Seasons Cotton, 2 skeins of Heart #209

materials

* U.S. size 8 needles or size needed to obtain gauge
* Pom-pom tree or pom-pom maker
* Scissors
* Yarn needle
* Ruler or tape measure

gauge

* 4 stitches per inch

Cast on 20 stitches. Work in garter stitch until the square measures 5 inches. Bind off. Cut the yarn, leaving an 8-inch tail. Pull through the remaining stitch. The tail will be used to seam the squares later.

FINISHING

When all of the squares are completed, lay them out on a flat surface to organize the colors. My main goal in creating a random patchwork pattern is to make sure no like colors are next to each other. I simply move the squares around until the layout is pleasing to my eye. For this design, I placed one square with the garter ridges running horizontally, and the next vertically. For the next row, reverse this pattern. That offers a more interesting texture.

With a yarn needle and the tail end of a square, sew the blanket together block by block with an easy whipstitch, with the right side of the blanket facing you. Seam whole columns together first, then seam the columns together.

Weave all of the ends into the seams on the wrong side of the blanket. Trim.

pom-poms • With the leftover yarn, make 28 pom-poms for the border. Make 4 pom-poms in each of the 7 colors from the blanket. Make 1-inch pom-poms with 30 wraps each.

Attach 1 pom-pom to each seam end and corner around the edge of the blanket, varying the colors.

baby sets

Although each of the pieces in this collection could certainly stand alone as an individual project, when they are all knitted and presented together as a set there is definitely a certain wow factor. You'll find something for every knitter and every baby here: sets for snuggling up to read a book with mom or dad, an embroidered outdoor jacket with mittens on a string, a colorful textured blanket with a matching hat and sweater, and the purest pure-white cotton layette set. It is all delicious and completely do-able!

I took inspiration from traditional baby sets that include a blanket, sweater, hat, and booties, and I shook them up by adding fun twists to those otherwise standard baby gifts. There is a bunny rattle, and a chubby bunny who adds an element of humor. I also added some great embroidery, interesting stitch-pattern work, and distinctive embellishments throughout the collection. It is a good thing to keep challenging yourself by adding new and interesting techniques along the way; who knows, maybe you'll find a new favorite in the following pages.

So pick and choose which projects suit you and the lucky baby's needs best and get those needles clicking!

circles and stripes stroller blanket

I love both the fall and the spring. There is something exciting about the changes those seasons bring that makes you want to get outside and walk with a baby. The air is crisp, clean, fragrant, and often a bit chilly; the perfect remedy is a hearty blanket to keep that baby snug as a bug. The beautiful organic cotton used in this stroller blanket is a luxurious treat with which to knit, and the natural colors lend themselves to this simple but interesting design. Made in four squares, this is a fairly quick and easy knit. The embroidered circles are a snap; the striped squares bring in a new, simple technique; and the cable border finishes the project off with style. Knit this one up quick and you'll be out walking in no time!

yarn

- Blue Sky Alpacas Organic Cotton (100% organic cotton; 150 yards/100 grams), 2 skeins each in Nut #82, Sand #81, and Bone #80

tools

- U.S. size 8 24-inch circular needle or size needed to obtain gauge
- U.S. size G crochet hook
- Cable needle
- Scissors
- Yarn needle
- Ruler or tape measure

gauge

- 4½ stitches per inch

finished measurement

- 34 inches by 31 inches

SOLID SQUARES (make 2)

With Sand, cast on 60 stitches. Work in stockinette stitch (knit all right side rows, purl all wrong side rows) until the square measures 15 inches. Bind off.

Repeat using Nut.

STRIPED SQUARES (make 2)

With Sand, cast on 60 stitches. Work in stockinette stitch, following the stripe pattern and using the sliding technique.

SLIDING TECHNIQUE FOR STRIPES • The colors of the stripes are changed every three rows. The reason a circular needle is required is so that when you have knit three rows and the working yarn of the next color is at the other side, you simply slide the stitches to the other end of the circular needles, carry the new color loosely up the side of your work, and start from there.

STRIPE PATTERN

3 rows Sand
3 rows Bone
Repeat.

When the piece measures 15 inches, bind off. Make a second striped square using Nut instead of Sand.

FINISHING

Sew the squares together using the mattress stitch, as detailed on page 150.

CABLE BORDER

With Sand, cast on 10 stitches. Work as follows:

Row 1: k2, p6, k2.

Row 2: Knit.

Rows 3–6: Repeat rows 1 and 2.

Row 7: k2, p6, k2.

Row 8: k2, slip 3 stitches onto the cable needle and hold to the front of the work, k3, k3 from the cable needle, k2.

Repeat rows 1 through 8 until the border measures as follows:

Side 1: 30 inches

Side 2: 32 inches

Side 3: 32 inches

Side 4: 34 inches

Bind off.

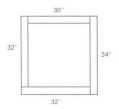

Sew the borders onto the corresponding sides using the whipstitch seam (see p. 9). Weave in all ends and trim.

> TIP • When making a border like this, I always check the length of the border against the length of the side as I go along to ensure that the border will fit before I bind off. I actually sew the border onto the side a bit at a time as I work.

embroidered circles

With Bone and the crochet hook, use the chain and wrapping stitch to form circles on the solid squares (see pp. 154 and 159). Use the photographs (above and on p. 29) as a guide or create a circle pattern that is pleasing to your eye.

circles stroller jacket and mittens

This cozy jacket feels like butter! It is soft and snuggly, and the circles add a subtle sophistication to the fabric that is wonderful. The optional fleece lining is what makes this a perfect outdoor jacket, but my children wear lined jackets indoors as well. It gets cold here in Wisconsin! Make sure to note the zipper-pull and hood details. The rings turned out great and add an unusual twist to the garment. The matching mittens on a string are the perfect way to use up the leftover yarn.

yarn

- Blue Sky Alpacas Organic Cotton (100% organic cotton; 150 yards/100 grams). Jacket: 3 skeins in Bone #80, 1 skein in Sand #81; Mittens only: 1 skein each in Bone #80 and Sand #81 (optional for the string)

tools

- U.S. size 9 needles or size needed to obtain gauge
- U.S. size 9 set of two double-pointed needles or size needed to obtain gauge
- U.S. size 7 set of four double-pointed needles for the zipper pull, hood rings, and the mittens
- U.S. size G crochet hook
- ½ yard of sherpa fleece material for lining (optional)
- Large piece of paper for lining pattern
- Pencil for tracing
- Sewing needle and thread to match lining
- 7 (8, 8)-inch separating zipper
- Four stitch holders
- Safety pins
- Straight pins
- Scissors
- Yarn needle
- Ruler or tape measure

gauge

- 4 stitches per inch (jacket)
- 5 stitches per inch (mittens)

sizes for the jacket and mittens

- 0–6 months (6–12 months, 12–18 months)

BACK

With size 9 needles and Bone, cast on 40 (44, 48) stitches. Knit 2 rows. Change to stockinette stitch, starting with a knit row, and work until the back measures 9 (10, 11) inches from the beginning. End with a purl row.

Next row (rs): knit across and place the stitches on three of the stitch holders as follows:
Stitch holder 1: 10 (12, 13) stitches.
Stitch holder 2: 20 (20, 22) stitches.
Stitch holder 3: 10 (12, 13) stitches.

RIGHT FRONT

Cast on 20 (22, 24) stitches. Knit 4 rows. Then work as follows:
Row 1: Knit.
Row 2: Purl to the last 3 stitches, k3.
Repeat rows 1 and 2 until the front measures 7½ (8½, 9½) inches from the beginning. End with row 2.

NECK SHAPING

Row 1: k3 and place on a safety pin, bind off 3 (3, 4) stitches, knit to the end of the row. 14 (16, 17) stitches remain.
Row 2: Purl.
Row 3: Bind off 3 (3, 4) stitches, knit to the end of the row. 11 (13, 13) stitches remain.
Row 4: Purl.
Row 5: Bind off 1 (1, 0) stitches, knit to the end of the row. 10 (12, 13) stitches remain.
Work even on the remaining stitches until the right front matches the length of the back. Place the stitches on a holder and set aside.

Cast on 20 (22, 24) stitches. Knit 4 rows. Then work as follows:

Row 1: Knit.

Row 2: k3, purl to the end of the row.

Repeat rows 1 and 2 until the front measures 7½ (8½, 9½) inches from the beginning. End with row 1.

Row 1: k3 and place on a safety pin, bind off 3 (3, 4) stitches, purl to the end of the row. 14 (16, 17) stitches remain.

Row 2: Knit.

Row 3: Bind off 3 (3, 4) stitches, purl to the end of the row. 11 (13, 13) stitches remain.

Row 4: Knit.

Row 5: Bind off 1 (1, 0) stitches, purl to the end of the row. 10 (12, 13) stitches remain.

Work even on the remaining stitches until the left front matches the length of the back. Leave the stitches on the needle for the three-needle bind-off shoulder seam.

The shoulders are seamed with a 3-needle bind-off, as detailed on page 149. Seam the stitches that are still on the needle from the left front, 10 (12, 13) stitches, and an equal number of stitches from the back left-shoulder stitch holder. Leave the remaining stitches from the back on the holders. Repeat for the other shoulder seam.

Only the body and hood of the jacket are lined. Lay the body of the jacket out flat on the large sheet of paper or newspaper. Trace around the back and fronts, adding a ½-inch seam allowance on the sides and at the neck edge. Cut the paper pattern out and set aside.

Measure down from the shoulder seam on the front and back 5 (5¼, 5½) inches, and place stitch markers or safety pins. With the knit side facing you, pick up and knit 40 (42, 44) stitches between the markers as detailed on page 145. Work 3 rows in stockinette stitch, starting with a purl row. Then work as follows:

Row 1: k1, ssk, knit to the last 3 stitches, k2tog, k1.

Row 2: Purl.

Row 3: Knit.

Row 4: Purl.

Row 5: Repeat row 1.

Repeat rows 1 through 5 another 3 (4, 5) times, until 32 (32, 32) stitches remain.

Work the following 2 rows 3 (1, 0) times:

Row 1: Purl.

Row 2: k1, ssk, knit to the last 3 stitches, k2tog, k1.

26 (30, 32) stitches remain.

Knit straight until the sleeve measures 6 (7, 7½) inches from the pickup row. Then work in garter stitch for ½ inch; the sleeve measures 6½ (7½, 8) inches from the pickup row. Bind off loosely. Repeat for second sleeve.

Sew the side and sleeve seams with the mattress stitch (see p. 150).

Starting at the right front, with the knit side facing you and leaving the 3 stitches on the safety pin, pick up and knit 8 (9, 10) stitches. For the back, pick up and knit 1 stitch, knit the 20 (20, 22) stitches from the back stitch holder, then pick up and knit 1 more stitch. Pick up and knit 8 (9, 10) stitches down the left front. Leave the 3 stitches from the left front on the safety pin. 38 (40, 44) stitches total. Purl 1 row.

Next row: (k4, m1) to the end of the row, knit any remaining stitches at the end. 46 (49, 54) stitches total.

Work in stockinette stitch until the hood measures 7 (7½, 8) inches from the pickup row. End with a purl row. For the 6–12 months size only, on this last purl row, begin the row by purling 2 stitches together (48 stitches remain). Divide the stitches evenly on two needles and turn the hood so the right sides are facing. Complete the 3-needle bind-off on the purl side as for the shoulder seams.

HOOD EDGING

With two size 9 double-pointed needles used as straight needles, knit the 3 stitches from the right front in garter stitch until the edging is long enough to fit around the front of the hood and meets up with the 3 stitches on the safety pin at the left front. Place the 3 stitches from the left front on a double-pointed needle. As detailed on page 151, use kitchener stitch to graft the ends of the edging together. Weave in the ends and trim.

CIRCLE EMBROIDERY

With the crochet hook and Sand, use the chain and wrapping stitch techniques to make circles along the bottom edge of the jacket, up the front edges, and around the hood. These are done freehand, so be creative and vary their sizes and placement.

lining (optional) • Lay the jacket on its side on a large sheet of paper, with the hood flat in profile. Trace the hood, adding a ½-inch seam allowance for the top and neckline seams. You will have to lift the hood as you trace the neckline, as it is already attached to the body. Mark the back of the hood on the paper pattern, as it will be placed on a folded edge of the fleece. At the front of the hood, trace the pattern so the lining will fall inside of the garter stitch edging. Cut out the pattern.

Lay the fleece out on a flat surface with one end folded inward just enough to accommodate the hood pattern piece with the back of the hood placed on the folded edge. Pin down the hood pattern to the folded fleece and the body pattern to the single thickness of fleece. Cut out both pieces. Assemble the body lining, either by

machine or by hand, by sewing the side seams together. Leave a ½-inch seam allowance. If sewing by hand, use the whipstitch to sew a ½ inch of the edges of the fleece together.

Sew the hood lining onto the neckline of the body and sew the top seam of the hood, leaving ½-inch seam allowances. When the hood and body of the lining have been joined, place the lining inside of the jacket, with wrong sides facing each other. Pin the lining into place all around the edges.

Using a needle and thread, sew the edges of the lining into the jacket around the front of the hood, down the fronts, across the bottom, and around the armholes by hand using the whipstitch.

ZIPPER

Pin the zipper into place on the wrong side of the fronts, with the top of the zipper ½ inch from the top neck edge. The zipper will not extend to the bottom edge of the jacket, but

that is fine. Turn the top ends of the zipper tape under so the folded edges are at the top neck edge. Be sure the zipper is inserted so that the front edges of the jacket will not catch in the zipper teeth when zipped. Stitch the zipper into place either by machine or by hand with a needle and thread using a backstitch, first along the front edge of the jacket close to the zipper teeth, then tack down the edges of the zipper tape to the inside of the jacket.

RINGS

zipper pull • With two double-pointed size 7 needles and Sand, cast on 3 stitches. Make I-cord (see p. 144) for 2 inches. Bind off. Cut the yarn, leaving a long tail, and pull through the last stitch. Thread the tail into a yarn needle and stitch the ends of the cord together to form a ring. With the remaining length of tail, tightly wrap the ring all the way around. Make several wraps go through the zipper pull. With the yarn needle, stitch under a few of the wraps and weave in the end. Trim neatly.

hood rings • Make the first ring the same as the zipper pull, but with an I-cord 2½ inches long. Make the last few wraps go through the point of the hood, attaching the ring to the hood.

Make a second ring the same way, with an I-cord 2 inches long. Before sewing the ends of the ring together, thread the cord through the ring already attached to the hood. Join the ends of the ring and wrap. Don't join this ring to the first ring; let it dangle freely.

MITTENS (make 2)

With four size 7 double-pointed needles and Bone, cast on 22 (24, 26) stitches onto 3 of the needles as follows:
Needle 1: 7 (8, 9) stitches.
Needle 2: 7 (8, 9) stitches.
Needle 3: 8 (8, 8) stitches.
Place a marker and join, making sure that the stitches aren't twisted.

Work in k1, p1 rib for 1¼ (1½, 1¾) inches. Change to stockinette stitch and work until the mitten measures 3 (3½, 4) inches from the beginning. Begin the decrease rounds for the top of the mitten:

DECREASE ROUNDS

Round 1: (k2, k2tog), repeat to the end of the round. 17 (18, 20) stitches remain.
Rounds 2 and 3: Knit.
Round 4: (k2, k2tog), repeat to the end of the round (knit the remaining stitch for the 0–6 months size). 13 (14, 15) stitches remain.
Round 5: Knit.
Round 6: k1 (0, 1), then k2tog to the end of the round. 7 (7, 8) stitches remain. Cut the working yarn and thread the tail into a yarn needle. Pull tail through the remaining stitches on needle and gather up tight.

Repeat for second mitten.

string (optional) • With the crochet hook and Sand, make a 28 (29, 30)-inch chain. Cut the working yarn and pull tail through the last stitch. Sew the ends of the chain to the inside of the mitten cuffs. Pull the string through the arms of the jacket so the mittens dangle from the ends of the sleeves.

BACK

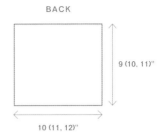

9 (10, 11)"

10 (11, 12)"

FRONTS

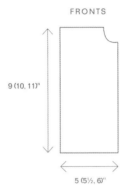

9 (10, 11)"

5 (5½, 6)"

HOOD

seamed together for top of head

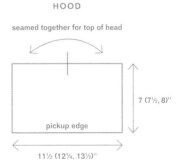

7 (7½, 8)"

pickup edge

11½ (12¼, 13½)"

SLEEVES

armhole edge

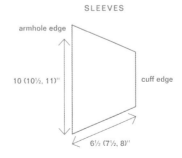

10 (10½, 11)"

cuff edge

6½ (7½, 8)"

chubby bunny

This chubby bunny came to me as a wonderful afterthought to the stroller blanket and jacket set. I had this gorgeous leftover cotton in the softest natural colors, and I knew I just had to make a toy to go along with the set. This bunny has character, and feels substantial to hold. I tried many different arms and legs on this little guy, but in the end the rings are the perfect match. I ran a strand of mohair through the body and limbs along with the cotton to add a bit of softness and a slightly fluffier feel. This is optional and it doesn't affect the gauge, so you can choose what works best for you.

yarn

- Blue Sky Alpacas Organic Cotton (100% organic cotton; 150 yards/100 grams), 1 skein each in Bone #80 and Sand #81
- Rowan Kidsilk Haze (70% super kid mohair, 30% silk; 229 yards/25 grams), 1 skein in Pearl #590 (optional)

materials

- U.S. size 9 needles
- U.S. size 5 set of five double-pointed needles or size needed to obtain gauge
- U.S. size G crochet hook
- One skein of black embroidery floss
- Stitch marker
- Small bag of polyester fiberfill
- Small bag of poly-pellets
- Scissors
- Yarn needle
- Ruler or tape measure

gauge

- 5 stitches per inch, using smaller needles

BASE

With two double-pointed needles used as straight needles and Bone and Pearl held together as one strand, cast on 5 stitches. Work in stockinette stitch as follows:

Row 1: kfb, k3, kfb. 7 stitches.
Row 2: pfb, p5, pfb. 9 stitches.
Row 3: kfb, k7, kfb. 11 stitches.
Row 4: pfb, p9, pfb. 13 stitches.

Rows 5–10: Work straight in stockinette stitch.
Row 11: kfb, k11, kfb. (15 stitches).
Rows 12–18: Work straight in stockinette stitch.
Row 19: ssk, k11, k2tog. 13 stitches remain.
Rows 20–26: Work straight in stockinette stitch.
Row 27: ssk, k9, k2tog. 11 stitches remain.
Row 28: p2tog through the back loops, p7, p2tog. 9 stitches remain.
Row 29: ssk, k5, k2tog. 7 stitches remain.
Row 30: p2tog through the back loops, p3, p2tog.
5 stitches remain.
Bind off, leaving the last stitch on the needle.

BODY

With the set of five double-pointed needles you will pick up stitches around the base. Starting with the stitch already left on the first double-pointed needle, begin picking up stitches until there are 13 stitches on that needle. Continue picking up stitches with each double-pointed needle going all the way around the base until there are 13 stitches on each of the four double-pointed needles. 52 stitches total. The fifth double-pointed needle is now your working needle. Place a stitch marker to mark the beginning of the round and join. Knit 1 round.
Next round: Increase 3 stitches on each needle as follows:
k2, (k3, m1) 3 times, k2. 16 stitches per needle. 64 stitches total.
Work straight for 2 inches from the pickup round. Begin the decrease rounds.

Round 1: (k6, k2tog), repeat to the end of the round. 14 stitches per needle remain. 56 stitches total.

Round 2: Knit.

Round 3: (k5, k2tog), repeat to the end of the round. 12 stitches per needle remain. 48 stitches total.

Round 4: Knit.

Round 5: (k4, k2tog), repeat to the end of the round. 10 stitches per needle remain, 40 stitches total.

Leaving the stitches on the double-pointed needles, chain stitch six circles in different sizes on the body with Sand and the crochet hook. With the yarn needle and a length of Sand, complete each circle, using the wrapping stitch (see p. 159). Weave the ends through to the inside of the body and trim neatly.

Round 6: Knit.

Round 7: (k3, k2tog), repeat to the end of the round. 8 stitches per needle remain. 32 stitches total.

Round 8: (k2, k2tog), repeat to the end of the round. 6 stitches per needle. 24 stitches total.

Round 9: (k1, k2tog), repeat to the end of the round. 4 stitches per needle remain. 16 stitches total.

Leaving the work on the needles, fill the bottom half of the body with poly-pellets, then stuff the rest with fiberfill until the body is firm.

Work in k1, p1 rib for 1 inch. Bind off loosely. Fold the ribbed section over in half, like a turtleneck, and whipstitch into place. Finish stuffing with fiberfill firmly up the top.

HEAD

With four double-pointed needles and Sand, cast 6 stitches evenly onto three of the needles (2 stitches per needle). Place a marker and join, making sure the stitches aren't twisted. Knit 1 round.

Begin the increase rounds.

Round 1: On each needle, k1, m1, k1. 3 stitches per needle. 9 stitches total.

Round 2: Knit.

Round 3: On each needle, k1, m1, k1, m1, k1. 5 stitches per needle. 15 stitches total.

Round 4: Knit.

Round 5: On each needle, k1, m1, k3, m1, k1. 7 stitches per needle. 21 stitches total.

Rounds 6–14: Knit.

Round 15: On each needle, k1, k2tog, k2tog, k2. 5 stitches per needle remain. 15 stitches total.

Rounds 16–17: Knit.

Round 18: On each needle, k1, k2tog, k2tog. 3 stitches per needle remain. 9 stitches total.

Round 19: Knit.

Round 20: On each needle: k1, k2tog. 2 stitches per needle remain. 6 stitches total.

Cut the yarn and thread tail into a yarn needle. Pull the tail through the remaining stitches. Stuff the head with fiberfill until firm, and pull the stitches tight to gather. Weave the end neatly to the inside of the head, and trim. Sew the head to the body using the whipstitch.

EARS (make 4)

With two double-pointed needles used as straight needles and Sand, cast on 6 stitches.

Rows 1–10: Work in stockinette stitch, starting with a knit row.

Row 11: k2, m1, k2, m1, k2. (8 stitches.)

Row 12: Purl.

Row 13: Knit.

Row 14: Purl.

Row 15: ssk, k4, k2tog. 6 stitches remain.

Row 16: Purl.

Row 17: ssk, k2, k2tog. 4 stitches remain.

Row 18: Purl.

Row 19: ssk, k2tog. 2 stitches remain.

Row 20: Purl.

Row 21: k2tog. 1 stitch remains.

Cut the yarn, and pull tail through the last stitch.

Make a second piece.

When two ear pieces are made, hold them purl sides together on top of each other. Thread the tail of one piece into a yarn needle and whipstitch the edges of the ear together. Pinch the bottom sides together, and sew for ¾ inch from the bottom. Sew the ear to the top of the head, using the whipstitch and following the photograph for placement.

Make two more pieces for the second ear, and repeat.

FACE
With black embroidery floss and the yarn needle, take small stitches for the eyes and nose.

ARMS (make 2)
With two double-pointed needles used as straight needles and Bone and Pearl held together as one strand, cast on 4 stitches. Work I-cord (see p. 144) for 2 inches. Bind off.

LEGS (make 2)
Work the same as the arms, but for only 1½ inches. Bind off.

HANDS AND FEET (make 4)
With two double-pointed needles and Sand, cast on 3 stitches. Work I-cord for 2 inches. Bind off. Cut the yarn, leaving a 12-inch tail, and pull through the remaining stitch. Thread the tail into a yarn needle and sew the ends of the I-cord together to form a ring. Tightly wrap the entire ring with Sand.

Once the ring is wrapped, wrap a few more times, going through the end of an arm or leg piece to attach. The feet are attached at a 90-degree angle so they stick up when the bunny is sitting. The hands are attached to hang straight down. Sew the legs to the picked up edge of the base so that the legs are sticking out in a sitting position. Sew the arms to the bunny at the start of the ribbing.

SCARF
With size 9 needles and Bone, cast on 4 stitches. Working in garter stitch, knit 2 rows in Bone, then knit 2 rows in Sand to form the stripe pattern. Continue knitting every row and switching colors every 2 rows until the scarf measures 4¾ inches. Bind off.

Sew the ends together around the bunny's neck, using the whipstitch, with the seam at the back of the neck.

POM-POM
With Sand and Kidsilk Haze held together as one strand, make a 1-inch pom-pom with 20 wraps. Sew to the back seam of the scarf.

flower cardigan and hat set

Simply constructed, this basic cardigan is so easy it is the perfect starter sweater for any knitter. By eliminating buttonholes and simplifying the shoulder and armhole seams, you can whip up this sweet flower cardigan in no time at all. The hat is quick and easy as well. To make this pattern more versatile, think about eliminating the flower and using I-cord loops for the button fasteners, or just using the flower center to make a few polka dots on the sweater. The cotton used for this set is an all-time favorite of mine. The colors are so vibrant, and the soft texture is luxurious to touch. This project radiates baby goodness all around.

yarn

- Manos del Uruguay Cotton Stria (100% Peruvian kettle-dyed cotton; 116 yards/50 grams). Cardigan: 2 (2, 3) skeins in Melon #205; Hat: 1 skein in Melon #205; Embellishments for the cardigan and hat: 1 skein each in Pistachio #204, White #211, and Tangerine #206

tools

For sweater • U.S. size 6 24-inch circular needle and set of two double-pointed needles, or size needed to obtain gauge

For hat • U.S. size 6 12-inch circular needle (for the two smallest sizes), size 6 16-inch circular needle (for the two larger sizes), and set of four double-pointed needles or size needed to obtain gauge

- Stitch markers or safety pins
- Two stitch holders
- Straight pins
- Scissors
- Yarn needle
- Ruler or tape measure

gauge

- 5 stitches per inch

cardigan sizes

- 0–6 months (6–12 months, 1–2 years)

hat sizes

- Newborn (3–6 months, 6–12 months, 1–2 years)

cardigan

BACK

With Melon, cast on 46 (56, 66) stitches. Work in seed stitch (see p. 142) for 8 rows as follows:
Row 1: (k1, p1), repeat to the end of the row.
Row 2: (p1, k1), repeat to the end of the row.
Repeat rows 1 and 2 three times more.

Change to stockinette stitch and work until the back measures 9 (11, 13) inches from the beginning. Slip all stitches onto a stitch holder.

LEFT FRONT

With Melon, cast on 23 (28, 33) stitches. Work 8 rows in seed stitch as for the back, then continue as follows:
Row 1: Knit to the last 3 stitches, k1, p1, k1.
Row 2: k1, p1, k1, purl to the end of the row.
Repeat the last 2 rows until the left front measures 7 (9, 11) inches from the beginning, ending with a knit row.
Next row: Bind off 3 (4, 5) stitches, purl to the end of the row. 20 (24, 28) stitches remain.
Knit 1 row.
Work the neck decreases:
Row 1: p1, p2tog, purl to the end of the row.
Row 2: Knit.
Repeat rows 1 and 2 until 15 (19, 23) stitches remain. Work even until the left front measures the same as the back. Place the stitches on a holder and set aside.

With Melon, cast on 23 (28, 33) stitches. Work 8 rows in seed stitch as for the back, then continue as follows:

Row 1: k1, p1, k1, knit to the end of the row.
Row 2: Purl to the last 3 stitches, k1, p1, k1.
Repeat the last 2 rows until the left front measures 7 (9, 11) inches from the beginning, ending with a purl row.
Next row: Bind off 3 (4, 5) stitches, knit to the end of the row. 20 (24, 28) stitches remain. Purl 1 row.
Work the neck decreases as follows:
Row 1: k1, ssk, knit to the end of the row.
Row 2: Purl.
Repeat rows 1 and 2 until 15 (19, 23) stitches remain. Work even until the right front measures the same as the back. Place the stitches on a holder and set aside.

The shoulders are seamed using the 3-needle bind-off (see p. 149). Place the stitches (15 [19, 23]) from the front on one of the double-pointed needles. Place the same number of shoulder-edge stitches (15 [19, 23]) from the back holder on another double-pointed needle. Leave the remaining stitches on the holder. Repeat for the other shoulder seam.

Now that the shoulder seams are finished, measure and mark with safety pins or stitch markers 4 (5, 6) inches down from the shoulder seam on fronts and back. With the right side facing you, pick up and knit 40 (50, 60) stitches between the markers. Start with a purl row, and work in stockinette stitch for 7 rows. Begin the decrease sequence:
Next row (decrease row): k1, ssk, knit to the last 3 stitches, k2tog, k1.
Work 3 rows, ending with a purl row.
Repeat the last 4 rows 3 (4, 5) times more. 32 (40, 48) stitches remain.
Work the decrease row every other knit row 1 (4, 6) times. 30 (34, 38) stitches remain.

Work even in stockinette stitch until the sleeve measures 4 (5, 5½) inches from the pickup row. End with a purl row.
Work 4 rows of seed stitch (see p. 142). Bind off loosely.

Repeat for the second sleeve.

Use the mattress stitch (see p. 150) to sew the sleeve and side seams. Weave ends in neatly and trim.

With Melon, and starting at the front right side edge, pick up and knit 14 (18, 22) stitches up the right neckline; knit 16 (18, 20) stitches from the back stitch holder; pick up and knit 14 (18, 22) stitches down the left neckline. 44 (54, 64) stitches total.
Work 3 rows of seed stitch. Bind off loosely.

Make 1 bobble in Melon and 3 (4, 5) bobbles in Pistachio as follows:
With two double-pointed needles used as straight needles, cast on 1 stitch *loosely,* leaving a 3-inch tail.
Row 1: kfb in the stitch until there are 5 stitches on the right needle.
Row 2: Knit.
Row 3: Purl.
Row 4: Knit, do not turn, pass the second, third, fourth, and fifth stitches over the first stitch.
Cut the yarn, leaving a 6-inch tail, and thread into a yarn needle. Stuff the bobble with the tail left from the cast-on. Gather up the edges of the bobble to form a ball. Use the 6-inch tail to attach the bobbles to the cardigan.

Place and attach the bobbles, sewing down firmly, on the left-side button band as follows:
0–6 months size: Place one Pistachio bobble 2 inches up from the bottom, then one 3½ inches and 5 inches up. Place one Melon bobble ½ inch down from the top neck edge.

6–12 months size: Place one Pistachio bobble 2½ inches up from the bottom, then one each 4, 5½, and 7 inches up from the bottom. Place one Melon bobble ½ inch down from the neck edge.

1–2 years size: Place one Pistachio bobble 3 inches up from the bottom, then one each 4½, 6, 7½, and
9 inches up from the bottom. Place one Melon bobble ½ inch down from the neck edge.

FLOWER

petals (make 5) • Have one extra double-pointed needle handy. With two double-pointed needles used as straight needles and White, cast on 3 stitches.
Row 1: kfb, k1, kfb. (5 stitches.)
Row 2: pfb, p3, pfb. (7 stitches.)
Rows 3–8: Work in stockinette stitch, starting with a knit row.
Row 9: ssk, k3, k2tog. 5 stitches remain.
Row 10: p2tog through the back loops, p1, p2tog.
3 stitches remain.
Cut the yarn. Place the 3 stitches on the extra double-pointed needle. Set aside.

Repeat until there are 5 petals, adding each new petal to the extra double-pointed needle. Make sure all petals are facing in the same direction. On the fifth petal, do not cut the yarn; instead, knit across the 3 remaining stitches and then knit across all of the stitches from the other petals (15 stitches total).
Next row: p1, p2tog to the end of the row. 8 stitches remain.
Cut the yarn, leaving a long tail, and thread it into a yarn needle. Pull through the remaining stitches and secure, but do not cut. Weave in the ends from the other petals on the back side of the flower and trim.

flower center (make 1) • With two double-pointed needles used as straight needles and Tangerine, cast on 3 stitches.
Row 1: kfb, k1, kfb. (5 stitches).

Row 2: pfb, p1, pfb. (7 stitches).
Rows 3–6: Work in stockinette stitch, starting with a knit row.
Row 7: ssk, k3, k2tog. 5 stitches remain.
Row 8: p2tog through the back loops, p1, p2tog. 3 stitches remain.
Bind off the remaining stitches. Using the whipstitch, sew the center to the petals.

Pin the flower to the right front, using the photograph as a guide for placement. Using the long tail remaining uncut from the petals and a yarn needle, sew the flower to the cardigan, using whipstitch.

stem • With two double-pointed needles used as straight needles and Pistachio, cast on 2 stitches. Make I-cord for 13 (17, 21) inches (see tip). K2tog on the last row. Cut the yarn and pull through the last stitch.

Using the photograph as a guide, sew the cord to the right front using the whipstitch, starting between two of the petals. Work out to the front edge of the sweater, then make as many loops as your sweater's size has bobbles. Each loop requires about 2 inches of cord. Make sure the loops aren't too loose, because you want the buttons to stay buttoned. The loops should fit snugly around the bobbles. Continue stitching the cord down all the way to the right bottom edge.

> **TIP** • When making a long cord like this, I actually sew it on as I go to ensure that I achieve the correct length. The length may vary slightly due to your individual knitting.

button loop • With two double-pointed needles used as straight needles and Melon, cast on 2 stitches. Make I-cord for 2 inches. K2tog on the last row. Cut the yarn, leaving a 6-inch tail. Thread the tail into a yarn needle and sew the loop directly across from the Melon bobble.

tassel • With Pistachio, make a 1-inch tassel with 10 wraps. Sew to the end of the I-cord at the right bottom edge. The ends of the tassel hang off of the edge of the sweater.

BACK

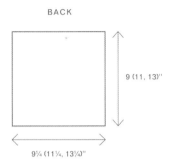

9 (11, 13)"

9¼ (11¼, 13¼)"

FRONTS

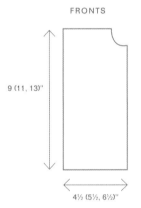

9 (11, 13)"

4½ (5½, 6½)"

SLEEVES

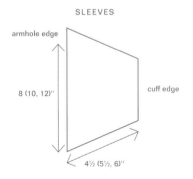

armhole edge

8 (10, 12)"

cuff edge

4½ (5½, 6)"

hat

With 12-inch circular needle and Melon, cast on 56 (64, 72, 80) stitches. Place a stitch marker and join, making sure the stitches aren't twisted. Work in seed stitch as follows:

Round 1: (k1, p1) to the end of the round.
Round 2: (p1, k1) to the end of the round.
Repeat rounds 1 and 2 until 6 rounds of seed stitch have been completed. Knit every round until the hat measures 4¼ (4¾, 5¼, 6) inches from the beginning. Start the decrease sequence.

DECREASE ROUNDS
Round 1: (k6, k2tog), repeat to the end of the round. 49 (56, 63, 70) stitches remain.
Round 2: (k5, k2tog), repeat to the end of the round. 42 (48, 54, 60) stitches remain.
Round 3: Knit.
Round 4: Transfer work from the circular needle to three of the double-pointed needles as follows:
Needle 1: (k4, k2tog) 2 (3, 3, 3) times. 10 (15, 15, 15) stitches on the first needle.
Needle 2: (k4, k2tog) 2 (3, 3, 3) times. 10 (15, 15, 15) stitches on the second needle.
Needle 3: (k4, k2tog) 3 (2, 3, 4) times. 15 (10, 15, 20) stitches on the third needle.
35 (40, 45, 50) stitches remain.
Using the fourth double-pointed needle as the working needle, continue working the decrease rounds:
Round 5: Knit.
Round 6: (k3, k2tog), repeat to the end of the round. 28 (32, 36, 40) stitches remain.
Round 7: Knit.
Round 8: (k2, k2tog), repeat to the end of the round. 21 (24, 27, 30) stitches remain.
Rounds 9–13: Knit.
Round 14: (k1, k2tog), repeat to the end of the round. 14 (16, 18, 20) stitches remain.
Rounds 15–19: Knit.
Round 20: k2tog, repeat to the end of the round. 7 (8, 9, 10) stitches remain.
Rounds 21–25: Knit.
Cut the working yarn and thread the tail into a

yarn needle. Pull the tail through the remaining stitches. Pull up tight and weave the end to the inside of the hat. Trim.

FLOWER

Make the petals and center as for the cardigan, and sew center to the petals.
Pin the flower into place on the hat, having one petal slightly overlap the seed stitch border. Sew the flower into place with the long tail from the petals. Weave in ends.

STEM

With two double-pointed needles and Pistachio, cast on 2 stitches. Make I-cord for 15 (15½, 16, 17) inches. Sew ½ inch of one end of the cord down with a whipstitch between 2 petals of the flower as in the photograph. Thread the other end of the I-cord into the yarn needle and stitch the cord through the hat about once every inch, spiraling the cord around the hat up toward the

point. The stem should make it around the hat once and come to the front again at the point. Make sure that the cord has a loose enough tension when threaded through the hat to allow for stretching. Sew the end of the cord down at the top point of the hat.

> TIP • I always measure I-cord as I go along, laying the cord out on the hat as I would place it when finished. The given measurements can vary slightly due to individual knitting tension.

TASSEL

With Pistachio, make a 1-inch tassel with 10 wraps. Sew this to the top point of the hat and secure the tassel to the hat so that it stands straight up.

baby's texture blanket

This fun blanket provides a lively baby with so many different textures to experience. The colors are brilliant, and textured stitch patterns, embroidery, and embellishments keep things interesting as you work. Combine the blanket with the Flower Cardigan and Hat Set (p. 38) for a fantastic gift.

yarn

- Manos del Uruguay Cotton Stria (100% Peruvian kettle-dyed cotton; 116 yards/50 grams), 2 skeins in Grape #202; 1 skein each in White #211, Bubble Gum #207, Red # 217, Melon #205, Tangerine #206, Pistachio #204, Aqua #210, Sky #209, Violet #210, and Lilac #208

tools

- U.S. size 6 needles or size needed to obtain gauge
- U.S. size G crochet hook
- Cable needle
- Stitch markers
- Scissors
- Yarn needle
- Ruler or tape measure

gauge

- 5 stitches per inch

finished measurements

- 32 inches square

> TIP • For projects that have many pieces to sew together, I always leave tails of about 8 inches when casting on and binding off. Later, I use the tails to seam the squares together.

PISTACHIO TEXTURED LINE SQUARE
(make 2)

With Pistachio, cast on 30 stitches.
Rows 1–4: Work in garter stitch.
Rows 5–8: Work in stockinette stitch, starting with a knit row.
Rows 9–12: Work in seed stitch (see p. 142).

Rows 13–16: Work in stockinette stitch, starting with a knit row.
Repeat rows 1 through 16 until the piece measures 6 inches. Bind off.

MELON BASKETWEAVE SQUARE
(make 2)

With Melon, cast on 30 stitches.
Rows 1–6: (k5, p5), repeat to the end of the row.
Rows 7–12: (p5, k5), repeat to the end of the row.
Repeat rows 1 through 12 until the piece measures 6 inches. Bind off.

AQUA SEED STITCH BORDER SQUARE
(make 2)

With Aqua, cast on 30 stitches. Work in seed stitch (see p. 142) until the square measures 1 inch from the beginning, ending with (p1, k1). Then work as follows:

Row 1: Work in seed stitch for the first 5 stitches, knit to the last 5 stitches, seed stitch to the end of the row.
Row 2: Work in seed stitch the first 5 stitches, purl to the last 5 stitches, seed stitch to the end of the row.
Repeat rows 1 and 2 until the square measures 5 inches from the beginning. Then repeat the seed stitch rows 1 and 2 until the piece measures 6 inches. Bind off.

SKY TWIST STITCH SQUARE (make 2)
TWIST STITCH

Knit in second stitch on left needle, leaving the second stitch on the left needle. Knit the first stitch and slide both stitches off the left needle.

With Sky cast on 30 stitches.

Row 1: (twist stitch, p1), repeat to the end of the row.

Row 2: (k1, p2), repeat to the end of the row. Repeat rows 1 and 2 until the square measures 6 inches from the beginning, ending with a row 2. Bind off.

BUBBLE GUM DROP-STITCH SQUARE (make 2)

With Bubble Gum, cast on 30 stitches. Work as follows:

Row 1: (k5, p1), repeat to the last 6 stitches, k6.

Row 2: p6, (k1, p5), repeat to the end of the row. Repeat rows 1 and 2 until the piece measures 6 inches.

Work the bind-off row as follows:

Bind off 4 stitches (drop the purl stitch off of the needle, place the top strand of the resulting ladder on the left needle from front to back, knit this stitch through the back loop, bind off 6 stitches); repeat to the last 7 stitches. Bind off 7 stitches. Pull all of the dropped stitches down to the cast-on row.

GRAPE SMOCKING SQUARE (make 2)

SMOCKING STITCH

With Grape, cast on 30 stitches. Work as follows:

Row 1: Knit.

Row 2: Purl.

Row 3: (k3, smocking stitch), repeat to the end of the row.

Row 4: Purl.

Row 5: Knit.

Row 6: Purl.

Row 7: (smocking stitch, k3), repeat to the end of the row.

Repeat rows 3 through 7 until the piece measures 6 inches. Bind off.

STRIPEY LOOP SQUARES (make 1 square with Tangerine and Bubble Gum, and 1 square with Tangerine and Aqua)

With Tangerine, cast on 30 stitches. Work as follows:

Row 1: Knit.

Rows 2 and 3: Purl.

Row 4: Purl.

Row 5: Knit.

Row 6: Purl.

Row 7: Purl.

Repeat rows 4 through 7 until the piece measures 6 inches. Bind off.

LOOP STITCH

With the crochet hook and Tangerine, crochet across the surface of the first purl row. Turn to go back across the single crochet row, creating loops as follows:

Put the crochet hook through the next single crochet. Wrap the yarn from front to back over your left index finger, making a 1-inch loop. With both strands at the bottom of the hook, pull both through the stitch. With 3 stitches on the hook, yarn over and draw them through all of the stitches. Repeat in each single crochet to the end of the row. Next, slip stitch in every stitch on the next purl row on the square, connecting the loop row with the next purl row.

Switch to either Bubble Gum or Aqua for the next loop row.

Repeat to the end of the square, alternating colors.

RED STOCKINETTE STITCH SQUARE (make 2)

With Red, cast on 30 stitches. Work in stockinette stitch until the piece measures 6 inches. Bind off.

WHITE SQUARE WITH RINGS (make 2)

With White, cast on 30 stitches. Work in stockinette stitch for 1 inch, ending with a purl row. The next row is the yarnover row.

Yarnover row: k5, (yo, k2tog, k4), repeat to the last 4 stitches, k4.

Work in stockinette stitch, starting with a purl row, until the piece measures 3 inches. End with a purl row.

Next row: k13, bind off 4 stitches, k12.

Next row: p13, cast on 4 stitches, p13.

Work in stockinette stitch, starting with a knit row, until the piece measures 5 inches from the beginning, ending with a purl row. Next, repeat the yarnover row.

Work in stockinette stitch, starting with a purl row, until the piece measures 6 inches from the beginning. Bind off.

embroidered rings • (follow the photograph for color placement, or make up your own!) With different lengths of colored yarn and the yarn needle, embroider straight stitches (see p. 158) around each hole in the square.

VIOLET CABLE SQUARE (make 2)

With Violet, cast on 30 stitches. Work as follows:

Row 1: p11, k8, p11.

Row 2: k11, p8, k11.

Rows 3 and 4: Repeat rows 1 and 2.

Row 5: p11, place 4 stitches on the cable needle and hold to the front, k4, k4 from the cable needle, p11.

Row 6: k11, p8, k11.

Repeat rows 1 through 6 until the piece measures 6 inches. Bind off.

STRIPEY GARTER STITCH SQUARE (make 5)

For all squares, with the specified color, cast on 30 stitches. Work in garter stitch until the piece measures 6 inches. Bind off.

stripe patterns • Make 2 squares in the following stripe pattern:

4 rows Bubble Gum

4 rows Pistachio

Repeat.

Make 2 squares in the following stripe pattern:

4 rows Violet

4 rows Lilac

Repeat.

Make 1 square in the following stripe pattern:

2 rows Red

2 rows Pistachio

Repeat.

FINISHING

Sew the squares together, using the photograph as a guide and the mattress stitch (see p. 150).

border

Side 1: With Grape, pick up 150 stitches (30 stitches per square) along one side of the blanket. Work in garter stitch for 7 rows. Bind off, leaving 1 stitch on the needle. Turn the corner for side 2.

Side 2: Leaving the 1 stitch on the needle, pick up 4 stitches from the border edge and 150 stitches from the second side (155 stitches total). Work in garter stitch for 7 rows. Bind off, leaving the last stitch on the needle. Turn the corner for side 3.

Side 3: Work same as side 2.

Side 4: Leaving the 1 stitch on the needle, pick up 4 stitches from the border, 150 stitches from the side, and 5 stitches from the border edge from side 1 (160 stitches total). Work in garter stitch for 7 rows. Bind off all stitches.

picot edging (same for all 4 sides) • With White, pick up 160 stitches. Knit 1 row.

Next row: (Cast on 2 stitches using the backward-loop method [see p. 143], bind off 4 stitches, slip the last stitch back onto the left needle), repeat to the end of the row, leaving the last stitch on the needle. Turn the corner and repeat until all four sides are edged.

flower (make 1)

PETALS (MAKE 5)

Have one extra double-pointed needle handy. With two double-pointed needles used as straight needles and White, cast on 3 stitches.

Row 1: kfb, k1, kfb. (5 stitches.)

Row 2: pfb, p3, pfb. (7 stitches.)

Rows 3–8: Work in stockinette stitch, starting with a knit row.

Row 9: ssk, k3, k2tog. 5 stitches remain.

Row 10: p2tog through the back loops, p1, p2tog.

3 stitches remain.

Cut the yarn. Place the 3 stitches on the extra double-pointed needle. Set aside.

Repeat until there are 5 petals, adding each new petal to the extra double-pointed needle. Make sure all petals are facing in the same direction. On the fifth petal, do not cut the yarn; instead, knit across the 3 remaining stitches and then knit across all of the stitches from the other petals (15 stitches total).

Next row: p1, p2tog to the end of the row. 8 stitches remain.

Cut the yarn, leaving a long tail. Thread the tail into a yarn needle and pull through the remaining stitches. Secure, but do not cut. Weave in the ends from the petals on the back side of the flower.

FLOWER CENTER (MAKE 1)

With Tangerine, cast on 3 stitches. Work as follows:

Row 1: kfb, k1, kfb. (5 stitches.)
Row 2: pfb, p1, pfb. (7 stitches.)
Rows 3–6: Work in stockinette stitch, starting with a knit row.
Row 7: ssk, k3, k2tog. 5 stitches remain.
Row 8: p2tog through the back loops, p1, p2tog. 3 stitches remain.
Bind off the remaining stitches. Sew the center to the petals, using the whipstitch. Sew the flower to the center of one of the red stockinette stitch squares, using the whipstitch.

bobbles (make 7) • Make 5-stitch bobbles in a variety of colors for the other red stockinette stitch square, as follows:
Cast on 1 stitch loosely in the desired color, leaving a 3-inch tail.
Row 1: kfb until there are 5 stitches on the right-hand needle.
Row 2: Knit.
Row 3: Purl.
Row 4: Knit, do not turn, pass the second, third, fourth, and fifth stitches over the first stitch.
Cut the yarn, leaving a 6-inch tail, and thread into a yarn needle. Stuff the bobble with the 3-inch tail left from the cast-on. Gather up the edges of the bobble with stitches to form a ball. Sew onto the red square with the 6-inch tail. Repeat until the desired number are made.

embellishments for the two aqua squares
FIRST AQUA SQUARE—LARGE CIRCLE
With Melon, cast on 3 stitches. Work as follows:
Row 1: kfb, k1, kfb. (5 stitches.)
Row 2: kfb, k3, kfb. (7 stitches.)
Row 3: kfb, k5, kfb. (9 stitches.)
Row 4: kfb, k7, kfb. (11 stitches.)
Row 5: kfb, k9, kfb. (13 stitches.)
Rows 6–15: Knit.
Row 16: ssk, k9, k2tog. 11 stitches remain.
Row 17: ssk, k7, k2tog. 9 stitches remain.
Row 18: ssk, k5, k2tog. 7 stitches remain.

Row 19: ssk, k3, k2tog. 5 stitches remain.
Row 20: ssk, k1, k2tog. 3 stitches remain.
Bind off. Cut the yarn, leaving an 8-inch tail, and pull through the remaining stitch.

SMALL LILAC SQUARE
With Lilac, cast on 6 stitches. Work in stockinette stitch for 1 inch. Bind off. Cut the yarn, leaving a 6-inch tail, and pull through the remaining stitch. Sew the square onto the center of the Melon circle with the whipstitch.

PISTACHIO EDGING
With the crochet hook and Pistachio, single crochet around the edge of the Melon circle, and join with a slip stitch.
Next round: (chain 3 stitches, slip stitch into the second stitch from the chain), repeat, attaching the chain to every other stitch.

Sew the embellished Melon circle to the center of one of the Aqua squares.

SECOND AQUA SQUARE—RED SQUARE
With Red, cast on 12 stitches. Knit every row until the square measures 2¼ inches from the beginning. Bind off. Sew the square onto the center of the Aqua square with the whipstitch.

PISTACHIO CIRCLE
With Pistachio, cast on 3 stitches. Work as follows:
Row 1: kfb, k1, kfb. (5 stitches.)
Row 2: pfb, p3, pfb. (7 stitches.)
Rows 3–6: Work in stockinette stitch, starting with a knit row.
Row 7: ssk, k3, k2tog. 5 stitches remain.
Row 8: p2tog through the back loops, p1, p2tog. 3 stitches remain.
Bind off the remaining stitches. Sew this circle onto the center of the Red square with the whipstitch.

cozy book pillow and slippers

This pillow has a wonderful surprise on the back—a pocket that is just the right size to hold a child's favorite book! Knitted simply in easy garter stitch squares, the pillow is great for both younger and older children. My ten-year-old daughter and twelve-year-old niece already have their requests in for a book pillow of their own. The cleverly constructed slippers also utilize garter stitch squares, rounding out a colorful and creative project that will be cherished for years to come!

yarn

- Blue Sky Alpacas Sport Weight (100% baby alpaca; 110 yards/50 grams), 2 skeins in Red #511; 1 skein each in Turquoise #532, Paprika #531, Chartreuse #527, Purple #529, and Amber #519

tools

- U.S. size 6 needles or size needed to obtain gauge
- 14-inch square pillow form
- Pom-pom tree or pom-pom maker
- Stitch markers
- Scissors
- Yarn needle
- Ruler or tape measure

gauge

- 5 stitches per inch, 12 garter stitch rows per inch, or 6 garter stitch ridges per inch

finished pillow size

- 14 inches square

slipper size

- 0–6 months (can easily be modified to fit larger feet, see pattern)

> TIP • You can always insert a zipper into one seam of the pillow cover if you are worried about washing or cleaning it.

pillow

BACK

With Red, cast on 70 stitches. Working in garter stitch (see p. 142), begin the stripe pattern.

STRIPE PATTERN

Rows 1 and 2: Red.
Rows 3 and 4: Turquoise.
Rows 5–16: Repeat rows 1–4.
Rows 17 and 18: Paprika.
Rows 19 and 20: Turquoise.
Rows 21–24: Repeat rows 17–20.
Rows 25 and 26: Paprika.
Rows 27 and 28: Chartreuse.
Rows 29–44: Repeat rows 25–28.
Rows 45 and 46: Purple.
Rows 47 and 48: Chartreuse.
Rows 49 and 50: Purple.
Rows 51 and 52: Amber.
Rows 53–60: Repeat rows 49–52.
Rows 61 and 62: Red.
Rows 63 and 64: Amber.
Rows 65–68: Repeat rows 61–64.
Repeat until the back measures 14 inches. Bind off. Weave in all ends and trim.

FRONT

The front of the pillow is constructed from four 6-inch squares, with a border added on later.

square version #1 (make 3) • With Purple, cast on 10 stitches. Work in garter stitch for 22 rows. Bind off all stitches. Cut the yarn and pull through the last loop.

Side 1: Referring to the earlier note, start at the last stitch of the bind off and work down the side, with Red, picking up and knitting 12 stitches. Knit 7 rows. Bind off, leaving the last stitch on the needle. Turn the square clockwise.

Side 2: Pick up and knit 13 stitches (14 stitches total are on the needle). Knit 7 rows. Bind off, leaving the last stitch on the needle. Turn the square clockwise.

Side 3: Pick up and knit 15 stitches (16 stitches total are on the needle). Knit 7 rows. Bind off, leaving the last stitch on the needle. Turn the square clockwise.

Side 4: Pick up and knit 17 stitches (18 stitches total are on the needle). Knit 7 rows. Bind off all stitches. Cut the yarn and pull through the last stitch.

Switch to Chartreuse.

Side 1: Starting at the last stitch of the row you just bound off, turn the square clockwise and pick up and knit 20 stitches. Knit 3 rows. Bind off, leaving the last stitch on the needle. Turn the square clockwise.

Side 2: Pick up and knit 17 stitches (18 stitches total are on the needle). Knit 3 rows. Bind off, leaving the last stitch on the needle. Turn the square clockwise.

Side 3: Pick up and knit 19 stitches (20 stitches total are on the needle). Knit 3 rows. Bind off, leaving the last stitch on the needle. Turn the square clockwise.

Side 4: Pick up and knit 19 stitches (20 stitches are on the needle). Knit 3 rows. Bind off all stitches. Cut the yarn and pull through the last stitch.

Switch to Turquoise.

Side 1: Starting at the last stitch of the row you just bound off, turn the square clockwise. Pick up and knit 22 stitches. Knit 1 row. Bind off, leaving the last stitch on the needle. Turn the square clockwise.

Side 2: Pick up and knit 19 stitches (20 stitches total are on the needle). Knit 1 row. Bind off, leaving the last stitch on the needle. Turn the square clockwise.

Side 3: Pick up and knit 21 stitches (22 stitches total are on the needle). Knit 1 row. Bind off, leaving the last stitch on the needle. Turn the square clockwise.

Side 4: Pick up and knit 21 stitches (22 stitches total are on the needle). Knit 1 row. Bind off all stitches. Cut the yarn and pull through the last stitch.

Weave in all ends and trim.

Switch to Paprika.

Side 1: Starting at the last stitch of the row you just bound off, turn the square clockwise. Pick up and knit 22 stitches. Knit 5 rows. Bind off, leaving the last stitch on the needle. Turn the square clockwise.

Side 2: Pick up and knit 23 stitches (24 stitches total are on the needle). Knit 5 rows. Bind off, leaving the last stitch on the needle. Turn the square clockwise.

Side 3: Pick up and knit 23 stitches (24 stitches total are on the needle). Knit 5 rows. Bind off, leaving the last stitch on the needle. Turn the square clockwise.

Side 4: Pick up and knit 25 stitches (26 stitches total are on the needle). Knit 5 rows. Bind off all stitches. Cut the yarn and pull through the last stitch.

Switch to Amber.

Side 1: Starting at the last stitch of the row you

just bound off, turn the square clockwise. Pick up and knit 28 stitches. Knit 3 rows. Bind off, leaving the last stitch on the needle. Turn the square clockwise.

Side 2: Pick up and knit 25 stitches (26 stitches total are on the needle). Knit 3 rows. Bind off, leaving the last stitch on the needle. Turn the square clockwise.

Side 3: Pick up and knit 27 stitches (28 stitches total are on the needle). Knit 3 rows. Bind off, leaving the last stitch on the needle. Turn the square clockwise.

Side 4: Pick up and knit 27 stitches (28 stitches total are on the needle). Knit 3 rows. Bind off all stitches. Cut the yarn and pull through the last stitch.

> NOTE • You should have a 6-inch square at this point. If not, you can add more rows around the edge.

square version #2 (make 2) • With Turquoise, cast on 10 stitches. Work in garter stitch for 22 rows. Bind off all stitches. Cut the yarn and pull through the last stitch.

Switch to Paprika.
Side 1: Starting at the last stitch of the row you just bound off, turn the square clockwise. Pick up and knit 12 stitches. Knit 1 row. Bind off, leaving the last stitch on the needle. Turn the square clockwise.

Side 2: Pick up and knit 9 stitches (10 stitches total are on the needle). Knit 1 row. Bind off, leaving the last stitch on the needle. Turn the square clockwise.

Side 3: Pick up and knit 13 stitches (14 stitches total are on the needle). Knit 1 row. Bind off, leaving the last stitch on the needle. Turn the square clockwise.

Side 4: Pick up and knit 13 stitches (14 stitches total are on the needle). Knit 1 row. Bind off all stitches. Cut the yarn and pull through the last stitch.

Switch to Red.
Side 1: Starting at the last stitch of the row you just bound off, turn the square clockwise. Pick up and knit 14 stitches. Knit 1 row. Bind off, leaving the last stitch on the needle. Turn the square clockwise.

Side 2: Pick up and knit 12 stitches (13 stitches total are on the needle). Knit 1 row. Bind off, leaving the last stitch on the needle. Turn the square clockwise.

Side 3: Pick up and knit 14 stitches (15 stitches total are on the needle). Knit 1 row. Bind off, leaving the last stitch on the needle. Turn the square clockwise.

Side 4: Pick up and knit 15 stitches (16 stitches total are on the needle). Knit 1 row. Bind off all stitches. Cut the yarn and pull through the last stitch.

Switch to Paprika.
Side 1: Starting at the last stitch of the row you just bound off, turn the square clockwise. Pick up and knit 16 stitches. Knit 1 row. Bind off, leaving the last stitch on the needle. Turn the square clockwise.

Side 2: Pick up and knit 14 stitches (15 stitches total are on the needle). Knit 1 row. Bind off, leaving the last stitch on the needle. Turn the square clockwise.

Side 3: Pick up and knit 15 stitches (16 stitches total are on the needle). Knit 1 row. Bind off, leaving the last stitch on the needle. Turn the square clockwise.

Side 4: Pick up and knit 17 stitches (18 stitches total are on the needle). Knit 1 row. Bind off all stitches. Cut the yarn and pull through the last stitch.

Switch to Red.
Side 1: Starting at the last stitch of the row you just bound off, turn the square clockwise. Pick up and knit 18 stitches. Knit 3 rows. Bind off, leaving the last stitch on the needle. Turn the square clockwise.

Side 2: Pick up and knit 17 stitches (18 stitches total are on the needle). Knit 3 rows. Bind off,

leaving the last stitch on the needle. Turn the square clockwise.

Side 4: Pick up and knit 28 stitches (29 stitches total are on the needle). Knit 5 rows. Bind off all stitches. Cut the yarn and pull through the last stitch.

Switch to Chartreuse.

Side 1: Starting at the last stitch of the row you just bound off, turn the square clockwise. Pick up and knit 27 stitches. Knit 3 rows. Bind off, leaving the last stitch on the needle. Turn the square clockwise.

Side 2: Pick up and knit 26 stitches (27 stitches total are on the needle). Knit 3 rows. Bind off, leaving the last stitch on the needle. Turn the square clockwise.

Side 3: Pick up and knit 27 stitches (28 stitches total are on the needle). Knit 3 rows. Bind off, leaving the last stitch on the needle. Turn the square clockwise.

Side 4: Pick up and knit 32 stitches (33 stitches total are on the needle). Knit 3 rows. Bind off all stitches. Cut the yarn and pull through the last stitch.

Switch to Turquoise.

Side 1: Starting at the last stitch of the row you just bound off, turn the square clockwise. Pick up and knit 30 stitches. Knit 1 row. Bind off, leaving the last stitch on the needle. Turn the square clockwise.

Side 2: Pick up and knit 28 stitches (29 stitches total are on the needle). Knit 1 row. Bind off, leaving the last stitch on the needle. Turn the square clockwise.

Side 3: Pick up and knit 29 stitches (30 stitches total are on the needle). Knit 1 row. Bind off, leaving the last stitch on the needle. Turn the square clockwise.

Side 4: Pick up and knit 33 stitches (34 stitches total are on the needle). Knit 1 row. Bind off all stitches. Cut the yarn and pull through the last stitch.

Switch to Purple.

leaving the last stitch on the needle. Turn the square clockwise.

Side 3: Pick up and knit 18 stitches (19 stitches total are on the needle). Knit 3 rows. Bind off, leaving the last stitch on the needle. Turn the square clockwise.

Side 4: Pick up and knit 22 stitches (23 stitches total are on the needle). Knit 3 rows. Bind off all stitches. Cut the yarn and pull through the last stitch.

Switch to Amber.

Side 1: Starting at the last stitch of the row you just bound off, turn the square clockwise. Pick up and knit 22 stitches. Knit 5 rows. Bind off, leaving the last stitch on the needle. Turn the square clockwise.

Side 2: Pick up and knit 23 stitches (24 stitches total are on the needle). Knit 5 rows. Bind off, leaving the last stitch on the needle. Turn the square clockwise.

Side 3: Pick up and knit 23 stitches (24 stitches total are on the needle). Knit 5 rows. Bind off,

Side 1: Starting at the last stitch of the row you just bound off, turn the square clockwise. Pick up and knit 31 stitches. Knit 1 row. Bind off, leaving the last stitch on the needle. Turn the square clockwise.

Side 2: Pick up and knit 30 stitches (31 stitches total are on the needle). Knit 1 row. Bind off, leaving the last stitch on the needle. Turn the square clockwise.

Side 3: Pick up and knit 31 stitches (32 stitches total are on the needle). Knit 1 row. Bind off, leaving the last stitch on the needle. Turn the square clockwise.

Side 4: Pick up and knit 35 stitches (36 stitches total are on the needle). Knit 1 row. Bind off all stitches. Cut the yarn and pull through the last stitch.

Sew the front together, alternating two Version #1 squares and two Version #2 squares. Use mattress stitch to seam the squares.

border

Side 1: With Red, and starting on any side, pick up and knit 60 stitches. Knit 7 rows. Bind off, leaving the last stitch on the needle. Turn the front clockwise.

Side 2: Pick up and knit 65 stitches (66 stitches total are on the needle). Knit 7 rows. Bind off, leaving the last stitch on the needle. Turn the front clockwise.

Side 3: Pick up and knit 70 stitches (71 stitches total are on the needle). Knit 7 rows. Bind off, leaving the last stitch on the needle. Turn the front clockwise.

Side 4: Pick up and knit 62 stitches (63 stitches are on the needle). Knit 7 rows. Bind off all stitches. Cut the yarn and pull through the last stitch.

embroidery • Using the photograph as a guide, embroider the center of the front squares using a variety of colors. With a strand of yarn threaded into a yarn needle, come up through the center of each square and use the split stitch (see p. 161) to make 3 stitches in a line as shown in the illustration *(opposite)*. Make eight spokes coming out from a center point. With a contrasting color, at the end of each spoke and in the center of the square, make a French knot as detailed on page 162.

FINISHING

Sew the seams on three sides of the pillow using the mattress stitch, and place the pillow form inside. Sew the last side together. To create the pocket, take the third Version #1 square and sew it to the back of the pillow using the whipstitch. Position the pocket however you prefer; the sample is sewn toward the lower left corner of the back.

tassels • Make four 2-inch tassels (see p. 153) with 30 wraps each in the following color combinations, holding two strands together:
Paprika and Turquoise
Amber and Red
Purple and Chartreuse
Chartreuse and Turquoise
Sew one tassel firmly to each corner.

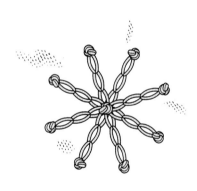

 Split stitch (p. 161).

 French knots (p. 161).

slippers

This slipper will fit a tiny newborn foot; if you want to make a larger version, just make a bigger square by adding on more rows in the same manner as the rest. Then make the sole wider by casting on more stitches (use an even number), and measure the length to fit.

UPPERS (make 2)

Make two squares in the Version #2 colorway and fold the square as follows:

1. Fold one corner across to meet the opposite corner, and sew the two layers of both open edges together with the whipstitch. This forms a triangle with one folded side and two sewn sides.
2. Hold the triangle with the folded edge down. Fold the triangle in half again so the two corners of the folded edge meet.
3. Sew 2¼ inches of the sewn edges together, starting at the folded edge corner. This is now the toe of the slipper.
4. Turn the back corner down to the outside, following the illustration, and stitch down at the corner to hold in place. This is now the top back edge of the slipper.
5. Make two 1-inch pom-poms (see p. 152) with 20 wraps each by holding a strand of Paprika and Red together. Attach them to the toe of each slipper.

SOLES (make 2)

With Red, cast on 18 stitches. Work every row as follows:
(k1, slip 1 stitch as if to purl with the yarn in back), repeat across the row.
Repeat this row until the sole measures 4 inches. Bind off, knitting 2 stitches together at a time as you work across the row.

Sew the sole into the bottom of the slipper top, slightly rounding the corners as you stitch.

Sample is a 6" square, but these could be made with any size square to create bigger slippers.

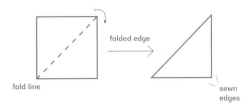

fold line   folded edge   sewn edges

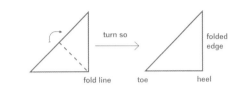

turn so   fold line   toe   folded edge   heel

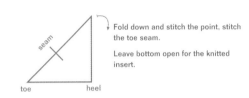

seam

Fold down and stitch the point, stitch the toe seam.

Leave bottom open for the knitted insert.

toe   heel

Bottom inserted and sewn in.

NOTE • The bottom is knitted as a separate piece.

cozy boatneck sweater

We all have a sweater that we love to cuddle up in, perhaps with a cup of hot chocolate and a good book. As adults, sweaters offer us homey comfort. I wanted to create a sweater for children that not only is beautiful, roomy, and cozy, but also evokes those comforting feelings. This boatneck design is easy to knit because it requires minimal shaping and seaming. Snuggle your favorite child into this little embroidered sweater with a favorite book to share, and spend some time just being together!

yarn

- Blue Sky Alpacas Sport Weight (100% alpaca; 110 yards/50 grams), 1 skein each in Red #511, Turquoise #532, Paprika #531, Chartreuse #527, Purple #529, and Amber #519

tools

- U.S. size 6 needles or size needed to obtain gauge
- U.S. size 3 needles or size needed to obtain gauge
- Stitch markers
- Scissors
- Yarn needle
- Ruler or tape measure

gauge

- 5 stitches per inch on larger needles

sizes

- Newborn (3–6 months, 6–9 months, 9–12 months, 12–24 months)

BACK AND FRONT

With the larger needles and Red, cast on 48 (50, 55, 60, 65) stitches. Working in garter stitch, begin the stripe pattern as for the Cozy Book-Reading Pillow on page 50. Repeat until the back measures 9 (9½, 10, 11, 12) inches from the beginning.

NECK OPENING

Continue in the stripe pattern, and work the following 2 rows:

Row 1: k8 (8, 10, 11, 12) stitches, bind off 32 (34, 35, 38, 41) stitches, knit to the end of the row.

Row 2: k8 (8, 10, 11, 12) stitches, cast on 32 (34, 35, 38, 41) stitches using the backward-loop method (see p. 143), knit to the end of the row.

Continue in the stripe pattern and garter stitch until the front measures the same length as the back. Bind off.

SLEEVES

Mark the shoulder on the sides of the sweater at the neck opening. Measure down from the marked shoulder 4½ (4½, 5, 5½, 6) inches on the front and back and mark with stitch markers. With Red, pick up and knit 44 (44, 50, 56, 60) stitches between markers. Begin working in garter stitch and the Stripe Pattern #1 as follows:

STRIPE PATTERN #1

Rows 1 and 2: Red.
Rows 3 and 4: Turquoise.
Rows 5–12: Repeat rows 1–4 two times more.
Rows 13–24: Red.
Rows 25 and 26: Paprika.
Rows 27 and 28: Chartreuse.
Rows 29–36: Repeat rows 25–28 two times more.
Rows 37–48: Paprika.
Repeat.

Knit every row for 1 (1½, 2, 2½, 3) inches from the pickup row. Begin the decrease rows.

Row 1: k1, ssk, k to the last 3 stitches, k2tog, k1.

Rows 2–6: Knit.

Repeat rows 1–6 until there are 32 (34, 38, 40, 42) stitches remaining.

Knit even until the sleeve measures 4½ (5, 6, 7, 8) inches from the pickup row. Switch to the smaller needles. Knit further for 1 inch or until the sleeve measures 5½ (6, 7, 8, 9) inches from the pickup row. Bind off loosely.

Repeat for the other sleeve using Stripe Pattern #2 and working the pickup row in Turquoise, as follows:

STRIPE PATTERN #2

Rows 1 and 2: Turquoise.

Rows 3 and 4: Chartreuse.

Rows 5–12: Repeat rows 1–4 two times more.

Rows 13–24: Turquoise.

Rows 25 and 26: Chartreuse.

Rows 27 and 28: Purple.

Rows 29–36: Repeat rows 25–28 two times more.

Rows 37–48: Chartreuse.

Repeat.

embroidery for sleeves • Use the photograph and the illustration (*right*) as a guide to complete the embroidery. There are six embroidered stars around the sleeve on each 12-row single-color section.

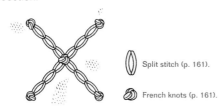

  Split stitch (p. 161).

French knots (p. 161).

SLEEVE #1

On the Red 12-row section of the sleeve, use Turquoise to work the split stitch and Chartreuse to work the French knots.

On the Paprika 12-row section of the sleeve, use Chartreuse to work the split stitch and Purple to work the French knots.

SLEEVE #2

On the Turquoise 12-row section, use Chartreuse to work the split stitch and Red to work the French knots.

On the Chartreuse 12-row section, use Purple to work the split stitch and Paprika to work the French knots.

patches (make 1 in red and 1 in turquoise)

With the smaller needles, cast on 10 stitches. Working in garter stitch, knit every row for 22 rows. Bind off.

embroidery

Work the embroidery using the split stitch technique and French knots in a contrasting color as described for the Cozy Book Pillow on page 50. Select colors of your choice. Whipstitch the patches to the sweater with the Red patch on the front lower left and the Turquoise patch in the center of the upper back.

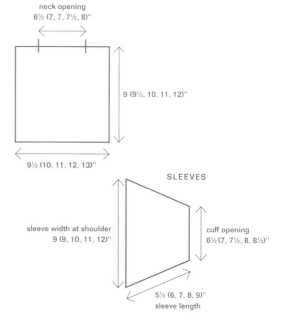

FRONT AND BACK

neck opening
6½ (7, 7, 7½, 8)"

9 (9½, 10, 11, 12)"

9½ (10, 11, 12, 13)"

SLEEVES

sleeve width at shoulder
9 (9, 10, 11, 12)"

cuff opening
6½ (7, 7½, 8, 8½)"

5½ (6, 7, 8, 9)"
sleeve length

pure and sweet layette

I am always struck by the total purity and innocence of newborn babies. To pay homage to this quality, I created the purest, sweetest layette set, one that is both simple and interesting, something beautiful to show off the exquisite new baby. Embellished with embroidery and stitch patterning, this little cardigan, hat, and booties are sized for newborns and babies up to a few months old, making it a perfect "take me home" outfit for this heavily documented event. And after the baby outgrows this ensemble, you might display it in a keepsake shadow box as a sweet reminder of a baby's first homecoming. A sweet bunny rattle and ruffle-edged blanket are included to complete this perfect newborn set.

yarn

- Rowan Handknit Cotton (100% cotton; 93 yards/50grams) in Bleached #263. Blanket: 8 skeins; Cardigan: 3 skeins; Hat: 1 skein; Booties: 1 skein; Bunny Rattle: 1 skein.
- Rowan Kidsilk Haze (70% super kid mohair, 30% silk) in Grace #580, small amount (for the Bunny Rattle nose)

tools

BLANKET

- U.S. size 7 24-inch circular needle or size needed to obtain gauge

CARDIGAN

- U.S. size 7 straight needles or size needed to obtain gauge
- U.S. size 5 straight needles or size needed to obtain gauge

HAT

- U.S. size 7 set of four double-pointed needles or size needed to obtain gauge
- U.S. size 7 12-inch circular needle or size needed to obtain gauge
- U.S. size 5 12-inch circular needle or size needed to obtain gauge

BOOTIES

- U.S. size 6 set of four double-pointed needles or size needed to obtain gauge

RATTLE

- U.S. size 3 set of four double-pointed needles or size needed to obtain gauge

- Small amount of black embroidery floss
- Two small circular bead containers and beads
- Super glue
- Polyester fiberfill
- Three stitch holders
- Stitch markers
- Straight pins
- Scissors
- Yarn needle
- Ruler or tape measure

gauge

- For cardigan, hat, and blanket: 5 stitches per inch on size 7 needles
- For booties: 5½ stitches per inch on size 6 needles
- For rattle: 6 stitches per inch on size 3 needles

ruffled blanket

finished measurement

- 30 inches square, including the ruffle

Using size 7 24-inch circular needle and Bleached, cast on 140 stitches.

Work in basket weave pattern as follows:
Rows 1–6: (k5, p5) to the end of the row.
Rows 7–12: (p5, k5) to the end of the row.
Repeat rows 1 through 12 until the blanket

measures 28 inches from the beginning, ending after either row 6 or row 12. Bind off, leaving the last stitch on the needle.

ruffle

The ruffle is worked separately on each side.

Turn the blanket so the right side is facing you and pick up 108 stitches, including the one stitch remaining on your needle, along one side as follows: (pick up 3 stitches, skip 1 stitch), repeat to end.

Turn and work as follows:
Row 1: k1, pfb in every stitch to the last stitch, k1.
Row 2: Knit.
Row 3: k1, purl to the last stitch, k1.
Row 4: Knit.
Row 5: Knit.
Bind off all stitches. Cut the yarn and pull through the remaining stitch to secure.

Repeat on the other three sides. With yarn threaded into a yarn needle, sew the corners of the ruffles together using the whipstitch.

> TIP • When casting on or picking up a large number of stitches, place a marker on the needle every 20 stitches to make it easier to count.

knotted cardigan

size

• 0–3 months

BACK

Using size 5 needles and Bleached, cast on 43 stitches. Work 6 rows in rib as follows:
Row 1: (k1, p1), repeat to the end of the row.
Row 2: (p1, k1), repeat to the end of the row.
Repeat rows 1 and 2 two times more. 6 rows total.

Change to size 7 needles and work in stockinette stitch until the piece measure 3½ inches from the beginning, ending with a wrong side row.

shape armholes • Bind off 4 stitches at the beginning of the next 2 rows. 35 stitches remain. Work evenly until piece measures 4 inches from the armhole, ending with a wrong side row. Place stitches on a stitch holder.

LEFT FRONT

Using size 5 needles and Bleached, cast on 25 stitches.
Rows 1–6: Rib as for the back. Change to size 7 needles.
Row 7: Knit to the last 4 stitches; place unworked stitches on a holder.
Continue working in stockinette stitch on the remaining 21 stitches until the piece measures 3½ inches from the beginning, ending with a wrong side row.

shape armhole

Next row: Bind off 4 stitches, knit to the end. 17 stitches remain.
Work evenly until piece measures 2 inches from the armhole shaping, ending with a right side row.

neck shaping

Row 1: Bind off 4 stitches, knit to the end. 13 stitches remain.
Row 2: Knit.
Row 3: p1, p2tog, purl to the end.
Repeat rows 2 and 3 four times. 8 stitches remain. Work evenly until the front is the same

length as the back. Place the remaining 8 stitches on a stitch holder.

RIGHT FRONT

Using size 5 needles and Bleached, cast on 25 stitches.

Rows 1–6: Rib as for back.

Row 7: Work 4 stitches in rib and place these stitches on a stitch holder. Change to size 7 needles and work in stockinette stitch for remaining 21 stitches, until piece measures 3½ inches from the beginning, ending with a right side row.

shape armhole

Next row: Bind off 4 stitches and purl to the end. 17 stitches remain.

Work evenly until piece measures 2 inches from the armhole shaping, ending with a wrong side row.

neck shaping

Row 1: Bind off 4 stitches, knit to the end. 13 stitches remain.

Row 2: Purl.

Row 3: k1, ssk, knit to the end.

Repeat rows 2 and 3 four times. 8 stitches remain. Leave the 8 remaining stitches on the needle.

From back, remove 8 right-shoulder stitches from holder and place on one of the larger double-pointed needles (leave remaining stitches on holder). With right sides of back and right front together and shoulders matching, complete a 3-needle bind-off for the shoulder seam (see p. 146). Repeat for left shoulder seam.

FRONT BANDS

Place the 4 left-front-band stitches from the stitch holder onto a size 5 needle. Work in garter stitch until band measures the same length as the front edge of the cardigan, to the neck edge. Place the 4 stitches back onto a stitch holder. Pin and sew the garter stitch band to the front opening of the cardigan with the mattress stitch (see p. 150).

Repeat for the right side.

> TIP • Sew the band onto the front as you knit to ensure that the band is the same length to the neck opening, using the mattress stitch.

NECKBAND

Using size 5 needles and Bleached, and starting at the right neck band edge, pick up and knit stitches along the neck edge as follows:

Knit 4 stitches from the right-front stitch holder; pick up and knit 11 stitches along the right-front neckline, 19 stitches from the back stitch holder; pick up and knit 11 stitches along the left-front neckline, knit 4 stitches from the left-front stitch holder. 49 stitches total.

Work 3 rows of rib as for the back. Bind off loosely in rib.

SLEEVES (make 2)

Using size 5 needles and Bleached, cast on 30 stitches. Rib as follows:

Row 1: (k1, p1), repeat to the end of the row.

Repeat row 1 for five more rows. 6 rows total. Change to size 7 needles and stockinette stitch.

Row 1: k1, kfb, knit to the last 2 stitches, kfb, k1. 32 stitches.

Rows 2–4: Work in stockinette stitch.

Repeat rows 1–4 until there are 40 stitches.

Repeat row 1. 42 stitches total.

Knit evenly until the sleeve measures 6 inches from the beginning, ending with a wrong side row. Bind off.

finishing sleeves • The sleeves are set-in style. The top of the sleeve is simply set into the armhole and the bound-off armhole from the body is sewn to the side of the sleeve using mattress stitch.

Complete the sweater by sewing the sleeve and side seams using mattress stitch.

KNOTTED CORD CLOSURES

(make 3 of each)

knotted cords • Using two size 3 double-pointed needles as straight needles and Bleached, cast on 3 stitches. Make I-cord (see p. 144) until piece measures 5 inches from the beginning. Bind off. Cut yarn, leaving a 6-inch tail, and pull tail through the remaining stitch to secure. Knot one end of each cord and sew the end down to the knot to secure, creating a ball.

loops • Using two size 3 double-pointed needles as straight needles and Bleached, cast on 2 stitches. Make I-cord until piece measures 1½ inches from the beginning. Bind off. Cut yarn, leaving a 6-inch tail, and pull tail through the remaining stitch to secure. With the yarn tail threaded into a yarn needle, whipstitch the loop ends together. Sew each loop to the left sweater front on the front band seam.

On the right front of the cardigan, pin the knotted cords to correspond to the loops on the left front. Place the loops as follows, measuring up from the cast-on edge: one loop at 2 inches, one at 3¼ inches, and one at 4½ inches.

With the end of a knotted cord threaded into a yarn needle, pull the cord from the right side through to the wrong side of the right front, next to the front band seam. Skip 3 stitches and pull the cord from the wrong side to the right side. Skip another 3 stitches and pull the end to the wrong side. Use the photograph as a guide. Sew the cord in place with the whipstitch. Invisibly weave in ends on the wrong side and trim. Repeat for the other three ball cords.

EMBROIDERY

Thread an 18-inch length of Bleached into a yarn needle and embroider a half circle of ½-inch straight stitches (see p. 158) around the loop. Then embroider another half circle of ½-inch straight stitches around the first half circle.

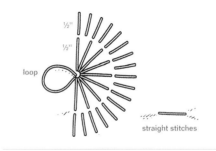

½"
½"
loop

straight stitches

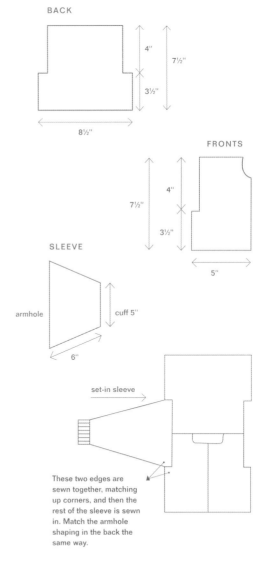

BACK

4"
7½"
3½"
8½"

FRONTS

4"
7½"
3½"
5"

SLEEVE

armhole
cuff 5"
6"

set-in sleeve

These two edges are sewn together, matching up corners, and then the rest of the sleeve is sewn in. Match the armhole shaping in the back the same way.

hat

Using size 5 12-inch circular needle and Bleached, cast on 56 stitches. Place a marker and join, making sure that the stitches aren't twisted. Work in k1, p1 rib until piece measures ½ inch from the beginning.
Change to size 7 12-inch circular needles and knit until piece measures 4 inches from the beginning.

shaping decreases

Round 1: (k6, k2tog), repeat to the end of the round. 48 stitches remain.
Round 2: (k5, k2tog), repeat to the end of the round. 42 stitches remain.
Round 3: Knit.
Round 4: Change to size 7 double-pointed needles and work as follows:
Needle 1: (k4, k2tog) 2 times. 10 stitches remain.
Needle 2: (k4, k2tog), 2 times. 10 stitches remain.
Needle 3: (k4, k2tog), 3 times. 15 stitches remain.
35 stitches total remain.

Continue knitting in the round as follows:
Round 5: Knit.
Round 6: (k3, k2tog), repeat to the end of the round. 28 stitches remain.
Round 7: Knit.
Round 8: (k2, k2tog), repeat to the end of the round. 21 stitches remain.
Round 9: (k1, k2tog), repeat to the end of the round. 14 stitches remain.
Rounds 10–14: Knit.
Round 15: k2tog, repeat to the end of the round. 7 stitches remain.
Rounds 16–18: Knit.
Round 19: (k1, k2tog), repeat to the end of the round. 4 stitches remain.

Place the remaining 4 stitches on one of the size 3 double-pointed needles. Make I-cord until it measures 3 inches. Bind off. Cut the yarn, leaving a 6-inch tail, and pull tail through the last stitch to secure. Knot the cord and sew the end to the knot to secure. Invisibly weave in the end on the wrong side.

embroidery • Using a 12-inch length of Bleached threaded into a yarn needle, embroider 8 straight stitches (see p. 158) fanning out from one center stitch like the spokes of a wheel. Randomly embroider five of these motifs on the hat.

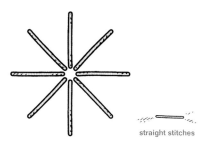

straight stitches

booties

CUFF

Using size 6 double-pointed needles and Bleached, cast on 24 stitches, distributing them evenly over three needles (8 stitches each). Place a marker and join, making sure that stitches aren't twisted.

Work in k1, p1 rib until the piece measures 3 inches from the beginning. Redistribute the stitches as follows:
Needle 1: 12 stitches.
Needles 2 and 3: 6 stitches each.

HEEL FLAP

Working back and forth on the 12 stitches on needle 1 only, work in stockinette stitch as follows:
Row 1: (sl1, k1), repeat to the end.
Row 2: sl1, purl to the end.
Repeat rows 1 and 2 once more. 4 rows total.

TURNING THE HEEL

Continue working on the 12 stitches on needle 1 only as follows:

Row 1: k6, k2tog, k1, turn work. 11 stitches remain.
Row 2: p2, p2tog, p1, turn. 10 stitches remain.
Row 3: k3, k2tog, k1, turn. 9 stitches remain.
Row 4: p4, p2tog, p1, turn. 8 stitches remain.
Row 5: k5, k2tog, turn. 7 stitches remain.
Row 6: p5, p2tog. 6 stitches remain.
Row 7: Knit.

SET UP FOR GUSSET

With the free needle, pick up 3 stitches along one side of the heel flap you just completed (needle 1). Combine the stitches on needles 2 and 3 onto one needle (this is the instep) and knit these 12 stitches. This is now needle 2. With the free needle, pick up 3 stitches along the other side of the heel flap and knit 3 stitches from the heel on needle 1. Place the remaining 3 stitches on needle 1. You should now have the stitches distributed as follows:

Needle 1: 6 stitches.
Needle 2: 12 stitches.
Needle 3: 6 stitches.

GUSSET

Place a stitch marker and knit in the round as follows:

Round 1: Knit.
Round 2:
Needle 1: k3, k2tog, k1. 5 stitches remain.
Needle 2: Knit. 12 stitches remain.
Needle 3: k1, ssk, k3. 5 stitches remain.
22 stitches total.

FOOT

Work in the round and knit every stitch until the foot measures 3 inches from the base of the heel.

TOE

Round 1:
Needle 1: k2, k2tog, k1. 4 stitches remain.
Needle 2: k1, ssk, k6, k2tog, k1. 10 stitches remain.

Needle 3: k1, ssk, k2. 4 stitches remain.
Round 2: Knit.
Round 3:
Needle 1: k1, k2tog, k1. 3 stitches remain.
Needle 2: k1, ssk, k4, k2tog, k1. 8 stitches remain.
Needle 3: k1, ssk, k1. 3 stitches remain.
Round 4: Knit.
Round 5:
Needle 1: k3.
Needle 2: k1, ssk, k2, k2tog, k1. 6 stitches remain.
Needle 3: k3.
12 stitches total.

Knit 3 stitches from needle 1 onto needle 3. There are now 6 stitches each on 2 needles. Break yarn, leaving a long tail, and thread tail into a yarn needle. Graft the toe closed with the kitchener stitch as detailed on page 151.

bunny rattle

With size 3 double-pointed needles and Bleached, cast on 9 stitches, distributing them evenly over three needles (3 stitches per needle). Place a marker and join, making sure the stitches aren't twisted.

body

Round 1: Knit.
Round 2: On each needle: k1, m1, k1, m1, k1. 5 stitches per needle, 15 stitches total.
Round 3: Knit.
Round 4: On each needle: kfb, k3, kfb. 7 stitches per needle, 21 stitches total.
Round 5: Knit.
Round 6: On each needle: kfb, k5, kfb. 9 stitches per needle, 27 stitches total.
Rounds 7–13: Knit.

Place enough beads in the small plastic bead container to make a rattling noise that is to your liking. Glue the container shut with super glue, and let dry. With yarn needle and Bleached, sew bottom hole closed. Place a small amount of polyester fiberfill in the bottom of the rattle, place the container on top of the fiberfill and continue to stuff around it. Resume knitting.

Round 14: On each needle: ssk, k5, k2tog. 7 stitches per needle, 21 stitches total remain.
Round 15: On each needle: ssk, k3, k2tog. 5 stitches per needle, 15 stitches total remain.
Round 16: Knit.
Round 17: On each needle: ssk, k1, k2tog. 3 stitches per needle, 9 stitches total remain. Knit straight until piece measures 3 inches from the beginning. Bind off. Stuff the rest of the body until it is firm, and set aside.

head

Repeat rounds 1–13.
Round 14: On each needle: ssk, k5 k2tog. 7 stitches per needle, 21 stitches total remain. Insert another plastic bead container as for the body, stuff around the container with fiberfill, and resume knitting.
Rounds 15–18: Knit.
Round 19: On each needle: ssk, k3, k2tog. 5 stitches per needle, 15 stitches total remain.
Rounds 20 and 21: Knit.
Round 22: On each needle: ssk, k1, k2tog. 3 stitches per needle, 9 stitches total remain.
Round 23: On each needle: ssk, k1. 2 stitches per needle, 6 stitches total remain.

Finish stuffing the head until it is firm. Cut the yarn and thread the tail into a yarn needle. Pull the tail through the remaining live stitches and pull up tight to create the nose. Weave the end to the inside and trim. Sew the head to the base,

making sure the base is completely filled before attaching it to the head.

scarf • With two size 3 double-pointed needles used as straight needles and Bleached, cast on 7 stitches. Work in garter stitch for 6 inches. Bind off.

Fold the piece in half lengthwise and whipstitch sides together. Wrap the scarf around the neck, and stitch it together to fit snuggly. Whipstitch the scarf into place around the top of the body.

Make two 1-inch pom-poms (see p. 152) with 20 wraps each. Attach them to the ends of the scarf.

ears (make 2) • With two size 3 double-pointed needles used as straight needles and Bleached, cast on 10 stitches. Work in garter stitch for 2 inches.
Last row: k2tog across the row. 5 stitches remain.

Cut the yarn and thread the tail into a yarn needle. Pull the tail through the remaining live stitches and pull tight to gather up. Fold the ear in half lengthwise and sew the sides together. Make a small crease in the bottom of the ear and stitch together. Sew the ears to the top of the bunny's head.

eyes and nose • With a yarn needle and black embroidery floss, take 2 stitches for the eyes. With a yarn needle and Grace, make several small stitches at the top of the nose.

nursery goodies

Boy, did I have some fun here! This is my kind of knitting. I had such a love affair with the projects offered in this collection for the nursery because they epitomize everything I think a nursery should be: a place of playfulness and stimulation, but also a place to feel safe and loved. Simply adding a handknit item to a baby's room is a nurturing act.

The Nursery Goodies collection offers a wide variety of projects for knitters who want something fun and different for a baby's room decor. I believe in mixing it up when it comes to color and theme; I don't think everything always has to match.

I created the Garden Mice Mobile with longevity in mind, because the mice can be taken off the mobile and used as stand-alone knitted toys or can simply be knitted as separate toys. The Baby Box Covers were knitted with function and practicality in mind. Tissues and wipes are a mainstay in every baby's room, so why not add a little style? The Clothesline can be personalized by adding your own knitted items or nonknitted memorabilia. Of course, every baby has to have Peas and Carrots in their life at one time or other! Hopefully these big, plush pillows will make every baby love their veggies.

Make some Nursery Goodies for the sweet baby in your life and I am sure you'll have the best-dressed nursery in town.

garden mice mobile

Unfortunately, my babies didn't actually spend much time, if any, in their cribs, and I know many other mothers who had the same experience. So I'll be honest here: I am not a big fan of buying an expensive mobile for a new baby, especially since it will have to come down in just a few short months.

With that being said, this is one of my favorite designs. I love these mice, and the reason I put so much detail into them is that after you take this mobile down from the crib, you can take the mice off of the mobile and play, play, play! It's a mobile that lives on long after its initial use. That's the best. These mice are fun to pretend with, or would be fantastic sitting on a bookshelf or in a basket in the nursery. My hope is to add usable decoration to the nursery for many years to come.

In creating this design, I simply went to a baby furnishings store and literally looked for the most inexpensive mobile I could find. The one I bought had little non-descript animals in diluted colors dangling from string. I stripped it down to the bare bones so just the plastic was left, then my needles started to fly.

yarn

- Blue Sky Alpacas Dyed Cotton (100% organic cotton; 150 yards/100 grams), 2 skeins in Tulip #615; 1 skein each in: Lemonade #608, Sky #616, Honeydew #602, and Azul #628
- Small amount of pink mohair for the noses. Sample is made with Rowan Kidsilk Haze (70% super kid mohair, 30% silk), in Grace #580

tools

- U.S. size 8 set of four double-pointed needles or size needed to obtain gauge
- U.S. size 7 set of two double-pointed needles or size needed to obtain gauge
- U.S. size 5 set of two double-pointed needles or size needed to obtain gauge
- U.S. size 3 set of four double-pointed needles or size needed to obtain gauge
- Mobile purchased from USA Baby and Child Space, model Rock-A-Bye (if you purchase a different mobile, take special care to measure the lengths as you knit)
- One skein of black embroidery floss
- One pipe cleaner
- Stitch markers
- Small bag of polyester fiberfill

- Small bag of poly-pellets
- Scissors
- Yarn needle
- Ruler or tape measure

> NOTE • This mobile came with a musical and spinning piece that hangs from the hook between the arm and the mobile. I removed this part, but you can leave it on the mobile if you wish to retain that element.

armature

ARM COVERING (for the arm that attaches to the crib)

gauge

- 4 stitches per inch

With Tulip and four size 8 double-pointed needles, cast on 24 stitches, distributing 8 stitches on each of three needles. Place a stitch marker and join, making sure the stitches aren't

twisted. Work 2 rounds of seed stitch as follows:
Round 1: (k1, p1), repeat to the end of the round.
Round 2: (p1, k1), repeat to the end of the round.
Continue, knitting every stitch, until the arm
cover measures 3 inches from the beginning.

Work 2 decrease rounds as follows:
Round 1: On each needle, k3, k2tog, k3. 7
stitches per needle remain, 21 stitches total.
Round 2: On each needle, k3, k2tog, k2. 6
stitches per needle remain, 18 stitches total.

Continue knitting every stitch until the arm cover
measures 10 inches from the beginning. Work 1
decrease round as follows:
On each needle: k2, k2tog, k2. 5 stitches per
needle remain, 15 stitches total.

Continue knitting every stitch until the arm cover
measures 20 inches from the beginning. Work 1
decrease round as follows:
On each needle: k2, k2tog, k1. 4 stitches per
needle remain, 12 stitches total.

Continue knitting every stitch until the arm cover
measures 24½ inches. Work 2 rounds in seed
stitch as above. Bind off all stitches. Slide the
covering over the arm of the mobile.

WINDING VINE

With two size 7 double-pointed needles and
Honeydew, cast on 2 stitches. Work I-cord
(see p. 144) until the vine measures 38 inches. Knit
the 2 stitches together. Cut the yarn and pull
through the remaining stitch. After winding the
vine around the arm 5 times, attach the top and
bottom of the vine to the arm covering with a few
stitches.

leaves • Make 22 leaves total, and place as
follows:
5 leaves for vine
9 leaves (3 per flower) for the top of the arm
4 leaves at the top of the center stem
4 leaves in between the mobile arms at the
center
With two size 5 double-pointed needles used
as straight needles and Honeydew, cast on

5 stitches, leaving an approximately 4-inch tail.
Row 1: k2, yo, k2tog, k1. (5 stitches.)
Row 2: Purl.
Rows 3 and 4: Repeat rows 1 and 2.
Row 5: ssk, yo, k2tog, k1. 4 stitches remain.
Row 6: p2tog twice, pass the second stitch over
the first stitch. 1 stitch remains.
Cut the yarn and pull through the remaining
stitch. Weave in the end to the back of the leaf.
Thread the tail from the cast-on edge into a yarn
needle. Gather up the cast-on edge by running a
couple of stitches through the edge and pulling
up tight. Sew the leaves onto the mobile as
instructed above. Begin by sewing five leaves
to the vine and attaching the cord to the arm
covering simultaneously.

mice (make 5)

I worked on these mice in an assembly-line
manner, making five bodies, five heads, and
ten ear parts. Then I assembled all of them,
including their faces, after I attached the ears.

gauge

• 6 stitches per inch

HEAD

With four size 3 double-pointed needles and
Tulip, cast on 9 stitches, distributing 3 stitches on
each of 3 needles. Place a stitch marker and join,
making sure the stitches aren't twisted.
Round 1: Knit.
Round 2: On each needle, k1, m1, k1, m1, k1.
5 stitches per needle, 15 stitches total.
Round 3: Knit.
Round 4: On each needle, k1, m1, k3, m1, k1.
7 stitches per needle, 21 stitches total.
Rounds 5–7: Knit.
Round 8: On each needle, k1, k2tog, k1, k2tog,
k1. 5 stitches per needle remain, 15 stitches
total.
Rounds 9 and 10: Knit.
Round 11: On each needle, ssk, k1, k2tog.

3 stitches per needle remain, 9 stitches total.
Round 12: Knit.
Tightly gather the cast-on edge into a circle and close using a yarn needle and the tail from the cast-on. Stuff the head with fiberfill until firm.
Round 13: On each needle, k1, k2tog. 2 stitches per needle remain, 6 stitches total.
Cut the yarn and thread the tail into a yarn needle. Pull tail through the live stitches on the needles and gather up tightly. Secure.

EARS (make 2 outer and 2 inner pieces for each mouse)
outer ear • With two size 3 double-pointed needles used as straight needles and Tulip, cast on 5 stitches.
Row 1: Knit.
Row 2: p1, m1, p3, m1, p1. (7 stitches.)
Row 3: Knit.
Row 4: Purl.
Row 5: Knit.
Row 6: p2tog, p3, p2tog. 5 stitches remain.
Row 7: ssk, k3, k2tog. 3 stitches remain.
Bind off purlwise.

inner ear (the inner ear is made in the color to match the stripes of the bodies; make one pair each in Lemonade, Honeydew, and Azul, and two pairs in Sky) • With two size 3 double-pointed needles used as straight needles, and a contrasting color, cast on 3 stitches.
Row 1: Knit.
Row 2: p1, m1, p1, m1, p1. (5 stitches.)
Row 3: Knit.
Row 4: Purl.
Row 5: ssk, k1, k2tog. 3 stitches remain.
Bind off purlwise.

Sew the inner ear to the outer ear by laying the smaller piece on top of the larger piece, with purl sides facing each other. With the tail of the inner ear threaded into a yarn needle, whipstitch the pieces together. Sew the ears to the top of the head, using the photograph as a guide for placement.

EYES
After the ears are attached to the head, use black embroidery floss and a yarn needle to take 2 small stitches for each of the eyes. Pull the thread through the head and snip so the end stays inside invisibly.

NOSE
You will make a small bobble for the nose. With two size 3 double-pointed needles used as straight needles and Grace, cast on 1 stitch.
Row 1: kfb until there are 3 stitches on the right needle.
Row 2: Knit.
Row 3: Purl.

Row 4: Knit, do not turn, pass the second and third stitches over the first stitch.
Cut the yarn and thread the tail into a yarn needle. Gather up the bobble and sew onto the mouse's face.

gauge

• **6 stitches per inch**

With four size 3 double-pointed needles and Tulip, cast on 9 stitches, distributing 3 stitches on 3 needles. Place a stitch marker and join, making sure the stitches aren't twisted. Work in the stripe pattern throughout the body as follows:

STRIPE PATTERN
2 rounds Tulip
2 rounds contrast color
Carry the colors along the inside of the body as you work.

Round 1: Knit.
Round 2: On each needle, k1, m1, k1, m1, k1.
5 stitches per needle, 15 stitches total.
Round 3: Knit.
Round 4: On each needle, k1, m1, k3, m1, k1.
7 stitches per needle, 21 stitches total.
Round 5: Knit.
Round 6: On each needle, k1, m1, k5, m1, k1.
9 stitches per needle, 27 stitches total.
Rounds 7–13: Knit.
Round 14: On each needle, ssk, k5, k2tog.
7 stitches per needle remain, 21 stitches total.
Round 15: Knit.
Round 16: On each needle, ssk, k3, k2tog.
5 stitches per needle remain, 15 stitches total.
Round 17: Knit.
Round 18: On each needle, ssk, k1, k2tog.
3 stitches per needle remain, 9 stitches total.

Stitch the bottom hole of the body closed. Stuff the body with poly-pellets until half full, then stuff the rest of the body with fiberfill until it is firm. Cut the yarn and thread into a yarn needle. Pull the tail through the live stitches and gather up tightly. Sew the head with the matching ears to the top of the body with a whipstitch.

hands and feet • With two size 3 double-pointed needles used as straight needles and a contrast color, cast on 8 stitches.
Rows 1–8: (k1, sl1 purlwise with yarn in back), repeat to the end of the row. Pull the needle out of the work and form the piece into a tube. Cut the yarn and thread the tail into a yarn needle. Draw tail through the live stitches. Turn the piece inside out so the knit side is facing outward. Gather the top tightly and secure. Weave in the end to the inside.

arms and legs • With two size 5 double-pointed needles and Tulip, cast on 2 stitches. Make I-cord for 2 inches, and knit the 2 stitches together. Cut the yarn and pull through the remaining stitch.

Sew the hands to the ends of the arms, and the legs to the top of the feet toward the gathered end. Sew the arms to the neck of the mice. Sew the legs toward the front of the body so the mouse can sit when not hanging from the mobile.

tails • With two size 3 double-pointed needles and Tulip, cast on 2 stitches. Make I-cord for 4 inches, and knit the 2 stitches together. Cut the yarn and pull through the remaining stitch. Sew the tail to the back of the mouse's body. Weave in any ends.

With two size 5 double-pointed needles and Honeydew, cast on 2 stitches. Make I-cord for 2 inches. Still working rows by sliding the stitches to the other end of the double-pointed needle, work as follows:

Row 1: kfb, kfb. (4 stitches.)
Row 2: Knit.
Row 3: kfb, k2, kfb. (6 stitches.)
Continue working a 6-stitch I-cord for a further 7¼ inches. Bind off. Slide the cover onto one of the mobile arms, with the 6-stitch cord end going on first.

Repeat three more times.

CENTER FLOWER (make 1)
petals (make 5) • With two size 3 double-pointed needles used as straight needles and Tulip, cast on 10 stitches.
Rows 1–12: (k1, sl1 purlwise with yarn in back), repeat to the end of the row. Pull the needle out and form the piece into a tube. Cut the yarn and thread the tail onto a yarn needle. Draw through the live stitches. Turn the piece inside out so the knit side is facing outward. Gather the top tightly and secure. Set aside.

When all five petals are finished, sew them together through their gathered tops to form a flower.

center • With two size 3 double-pointed needles used as straight needles and Azul, cast on 1 stitch loosely, leaving a 3-inch tail.
Row 1: kfb in the stitch until there are 5 stitches on the right needle.
Row 2: Knit.
Row 3: Purl.
Row 4: Knit, do not turn; pass the second, third, fourth, and fifth stitches over the first stitch. Cut the yarn, leaving a 6-inch tail, and thread into a yarn needle. Stuff the bobble with the tail left from the cast-on. Gather up the edges of the bobble to create a ball and sew the bobble to the center of the flower. Pull the tail through to the inside of the bobble and cut the tail so it stays inside.

center stem • With two size 5 double-pointed needles used as straight needles and Honeydew, cast on 4 stitches. Work I-cord for 7 inches. Bind off. Cut the yarn, leaving a 6-inch tail. Stuff the I-cord with the pipe cleaner, bending the sharp tip of the pipe cleaner into a tight loop before stuffing it into the cord so it doesn't catch on the stitches. Trim any remaining piece of the pipe cleaner that hangs out of the end of the cord.

Sew the cast-on end of the stem to the back of the center flower. Twist the stem loosely around a size 8 double-pointed needle and pull the needle out gently. Sew the end of the stem to the hook at the center of the mobile.

Sew four leaves to the top of the stem to hide the hook.

petals (make 5 per flower) • With two size 3 double-pointed needles used as straight needles and Tulip, cast on 8 stitches.
Rows 1–10: (k1, sl1 purlwise with yarn in back), repeat to the end of the row. Pull the needle out and form the piece into a tube. Cut the yarn and thread tail into a yarn needle. Draw through the live stitches. Turn the piece inside out so the knit side is facing outward. Gather up the top tightly and secure. Set aside.

When all five petals are finished, sew them together through their gathered ends to form a flower.

centers (make 2 in Azul, 2 in Honeydew, 2 in Lemonade, and 1 in Sky) • With two size 3 double-pointed needles used as straight needles and a contrast color, cast on 1 stitch loosely, leaving a 3-inch end.
Row 1: kfb until there are 5 stitches on the right needle.
Row 2: Knit.
Row 3: Purl.
Row 4: Knit, do not turn; pass the second, third, fourth, and fifth stitches over the first stitch. Cut the yarn, leaving a 6-inch tail, and thread into a yarn needle. Stuff the bobble with the tail left from the cast-on. Gather up the edges of the bobble to create a ball and sew to the center of the flower. Pull the tail through to the inside of the bobble and cut the tail so it stays inside.

Sew four of the flowers (one in each center color) to the ends of the I-cords, with the centers facing down. Sew the three remaining flowers to the top end of the arm covering so it hides the hook. Sew three leaves around the back of each of these flowers (nine leaves total).

Sew the last four leaves between the mobile arms, connecting the cords and covering up any visible plastic. This will secure the cords so that they can't be pulled off. Sew the mice hanging in different ways from the center of the flowers at the ends of the mobile arms as follows:
Lemonade mouse: hanging from the left foot only.
Azul mouse: hanging from both hands.
Sky mouse: hanging from the right hand only.
Honeydew mouse: hanging from the tail only.
The last Sky mouse is meant to sit on top of the mobile. To attach him, sew him directly onto the arm covering. To make the mouse extra secure, run stitches through the bottom of the mouse and inside the arm covering, around the plastic arm, so you can't see the stitches from the outside.

baby box covers

My just slightly older and vastly wiser sister, Dawn, and I each have four children. I look to her for advice on just about everything, but especially when it comes to the kids. She has daughters who are older than my oldest son, so she sure knows the ropes. For this project, I wanted to knit some box covers for standard changing table and dresser items, and asked Dawn what items one *really* needs in the nursery. We both came to the conclusion that the two mainstays of the nursery are a box of tissues and a box of wipes. That's really it.

I wanted to make these boxes as cute as can be. The tissue box will always be around the child's room, and the wipes box will be around for several years, so why not make them look fun and whimsical? These are quick-knit projects that would make terrific gifts for any mom!

I am very excited about the new dots I used on these boxes. I love polka dots, but I didn't want to do the same old dots I've used before. I came up with an embroidered woven stitch that turned out fantastically. The technique is fairly quick and adds textural interest to the knitted fabric. Take the time to practice making them and you can use these dots everywhere!

The yarn, tools, and gauge are the same for both of the boxes.

yarn

- Blue Sky Alpacas Dyed Cotton (100% organic cotton; 150 yards/100 grams), 1 skein each in Lemonade #608, Tulip #615, Sky #616, Honeydew #602, and Azul #628

tools

- U.S. size 7 needles or size needed to obtain gauge
- U.S. size G crochet hook
- Luvs brand wipes with the pop-up top
- Square tissue box
- Stitch holder (for tissue box only)
- Pom-pom tree or pom-pom maker
- Scissors
- Yarn needle
- Ruler or tape measure

gauge

- 5 stitches per inch

TIP • I used the leftover yarn from the Garden Mice Mobile to make these two box covers. It is a great way to use up oddball yarn, and as an added bonus, the projects match!

dotted wipes box

ENDS (make 2)

With size 7 needles and Lemonade, cast on 25 stitches and work 4 rows in garter stitch. Then work in stockinette stitch until the piece measures 3½ inches from the beginning. End with a right side row. Work 5 rows in garter stitch. Bind off all stitches.

With size 7 needles and Lemonade, cast on
35 stitches. Work as for the ends.

Sew the four sides together using mattress stitch
to form a rectangular box.

With size 7 needles and Lemonade, cast on
5 stitches. Work in garter stitch until the strap
measures 4 inches. Bind off.

Sew the pieces on the top of the box on either
side of the pop-up top. Sew the side of the piece
to the end of the box and the cast-on edge and
bound-off edge to the front and back of the box.

These embellishments are worked freehand. With
the crochet hook, yarn needle, and Honeydew,
Tulip, Sky, and Azul, embroider the dots in
various sizes around the four sides, following the
instructions on page 160.

Create as many dots as you desire on each side.
The sample has five dots on the front and back,
and two dots on each of the ends.

Make four 2-inch pom-poms with 40 wraps
in Tulip, Honeydew, and Azul, following the
instructions on page 152. Make six pom-poms
in Sky. Attach four pom-poms, one of each color,
on both sides of the box along the top seams.
Attach five pom-poms, one of each color and

an extra one in Sky, along the front and back of the box just below the garter stitch border. Attach by pulling the long ends from the pom-pom tie through to the wrong side and tying a knot. Trim all ends.

dotted tissue box

SIDES (make 4)

With size 7 needles and Tulip, cast on 25 stitches. Work in seed stitch until the side measures 5 inches. Bind off.

With mattress stitch sew the four sides together to create a box. Pinch together ½ inch on either side of the seam to form a ridge. Use a length of Tulip and a yarn needle to sew the ridge together using the backstitch (see p. 156). Repeat on each corner.

TOP

With size 7 needles and Tulip, cast on 19 stitches. Work as follows:
Row 1: (k1, p1), repeat to the end of the row.
Rows 2–8: Repeat row 1.
Row 9: k8 and place on a stitch holder, bind off 3 stitches, k8. 16 stitches remain.
Row 10: Working on the first 8 stitches only, seed stitch to the end of the row.
Row 11: ssk, seed stitch to the end of the row. 7 stitches remain.
Row 12: Seed stitch to the end of the row.
Row 13: ssk, seed stitch to the end of the row. 6 stitches remain.
Rows 14–22: Seed stitch all rows.
Row 23: kfb, seed stitch to the end of the row. (7 stitches.)
Row 24: Seed stitch.
Row 25: kfb, seed stitch to the end of the row. (8 stitches.)

Place these 8 stitches on a stitch holder.

Reattach the yarn at the center opening. Place the other set of 8 stitches on the needle and work as follows:
Row 1: Seed stitch.
Row 2: Seed stitch to the last 2 stitches, k2tog. 7 stitches remain.
Row 3: Seed stitch.
Row 4: Seed stitch to the last 2 stitches, k2tog. 6 stitches remain.
Rows 5–13: Seed stitch.
Row 14: Seed stitch to the last stitch, kfb. (7 stitches.)
Row 15: Seed stitch.
Row 16: Seed stitch to the last stitch, kfb. (8 stitches.)
Row 17: Seed stitch.
Row 18: Seed stitch across 8 stitches, cast on 3 stitches, place the first set of 8 stitches back on the needle, and seed stitch across them. There are 19 stitches on your needle.
Rows 19–26: Seed stitch.
Bind off all stitches.

With the crochet hook and Lemonade, work single crochet around the opening in the box top. Sew the top to the four sides with whipstitch.

WOVEN DOTS

The woven dots for the tissue box are the same as those used for the wipes box cover. The tissue box has three to four dots on each side.

POM-POMS (make 6)

Make two 2-inch pom-poms, with 40 wraps in Lemonade, Honeydew, and Sky. Attach the pom-poms around the opening in the box top according to the instructions for the Dotted Wipes Box.

clothesline

I use knitted items as pieces of art all over my house to liven things up in a playful way. This clothesline is a terrific way to create knitted art in a child's room. The four clothing items hung on the line are colorful and happy, and the parasol adds whimsy. You might also hang a child's photo, a little knitted animal, or any other fun items you find!

I love the yarns used here. Rowan's Summer Tweed, which I used to knit the two sweaters and to embroider the jeans, is a treat to work with because it softens up as you knit. Noro Sakura, used as trim on the short-sleeved sweater and for the skirt, is a newer addition to the company's product line. The wrapped sections remind me of the fun, colorful hair wraps worked with embroidery floss girls love to make in their hair. (Have you seen those?) Of course, Rowan's Denim is one of my all-time favorite yarns, one I couldn't omit from this clothesline. After all, what clothesline would be complete without a pair of jeans?

yarn

- Rowan Summer Tweed (70% silk, 30% cotton; 118 yards/50 grams), 1 skein each in Bouquet #510 and Brilliant #528
- Rowan Denim (100% cotton; 102 yards/50 grams), 1 skein in Tennessee #231
- Noro Sakura (36% rayon, 28% polyester, 18% nylon, 11% silk, 7% lamb's wool; 147 yards/40 grams), 1 skein in #6
- turtleneck sweater: Bouquet and Brilliant
- t-shirt: Brilliant and Sakura
- jeans: Tennessee and Brilliant
- skirt: Sakura
- parasol and finials: Brilliant, Bouquet, Tennessee, and Sakura

tools

- U.S. size 8 double-pointed needles or size needed to obtain gauge
- U.S. size 6 double-pointed needles or size needed to obtain gauge
- U.S. size 3 double-pointed needles or size needed to obtain gauge
- U.S. size G crochet hook
- 4 feet of 0 gauge flexible wire
- 10 mini clothespins, Cavallini & Co. Can o' Clips
- Small bag of polyester fiberfill
- 20 inches of ½-inch-wide ribbon
- Stitch markers
- Stitch holders
- Scissors
- Yarn needle
- Ruler or tape measure

gauge

- Rowan Summer Tweed: 4 stitches per inch on size 8 needles
- Noro Sakura: 4 stitches per inch on size 8 needles
- Rowan Denim, Rowan Summer Tweed: 5 stitches per inch on size 6 needles

finished measurements

- All pieces are 5 to 6 inches in length

turtleneck sweater

BODY

Using two size 8 double-pointed needles as straight needles and Bouquet, cast on 24 stitches. Work in k2, p2 rib for 4 rows. Work in stockinette stitch until piece measures 6 inches from the beginning.

Next row (neck opening): k6, bind off 12 stitches. 12 stitches remain. Knit to the end of the row.

Next row: p6, cast on 12 stitches using backward-loop method (see p. 143), p6. (24 stitches.)

Continue working in stockinette stitch until piece measures 11¼ inches from the beginning. Work 4 rows in k2, p2 rib. Bind off in rib.

COLLAR

Using 4 size 8 double-pointed needles, pick up 32 stitches around neck edge as follows:

Needles 1 and 2: 10 stitches per needle.

Needle 3: 12 stitches.

Work in the round in k2, p2 rib for 2 inches. Bind off loosely in rib.

SLEEVES

Measure and mark 3½ inches from the bottom edges on both sides of front and back. Using two size 8 double-pointed needles as straight needles with right side facing you, pick up 24 stitches between the markers on one side edge. Starting with a purl row, work in stockinette stitch until sleeve measures ¾ of an inch, ending on wrong side row. Begin decreases:

Row 1: ssk, knit to last 2 stitches, k2tog. 22 stitches remain.

Row 2: Purl.

Row 3: Knit.

Row 4: Purl.

Repeat rows 1–4 until 16 stitches remain and work measures 3¾ inches from the beginning. Work in k2, p2 rib for 4 rows. Bind off loosely in rib.

Repeat on other side.

FINISHING

Fold piece in half and sew side and sleeve seams using mattress stitch.

t-shirt

FRONT AND BACK

Using two size 8 double-pointed needles as straight needles and Brilliant, cast on 24 stitches. Work in k2, p2 rib until piece measures 5 inches.

Next row: Work in rib for 12 stitches. Place remaining stitches on a stitch holder.

Turn, and working only those 12 stitches:

Row 1: ssk, rib to end. 11 stitches remain.

Row 2: Rib to last 2 stitches, k2tog. 10 stitches remain.

Row 3: p2tog, rib to last 2 stitches. 9 stitches remain.

Row 4: Rib to last 2 stitches, k2tog. 8 stitches remain.

Row 5: ssk, rib to end. 7 stitches remain.

Row 6: Work to end, k2tog. 6 stitches remain.

Break yarn. Rejoin yarn at center and working only on 12 stitches from holder repeat rows 1 through 6 for the other side.

Next row: Rib across.

Next row: Rib 6 stitches, cast on 12 stitches using the backward-loop method, rib 6 stitches. (24 stitches.)

Continue working in rib until back matches front, measuring 12 inches total from the cast-on edge. Bind off loosely in rib.

SLEEVES

Measure and mark 3½ inches from the bottom edges on both edges of front and back. Using two size 8 double-pointed needles as straight needles and Brilliant with right side facing you, pick up 24 stitches between the markers on one side edge. Starting with a purl row, work in k2, p2 rib until sleeve measures ¾ of an inch from the beginning, ending on a wrong side row.

Row 1: ssk, rib to last 2 stitches, k2tog. 22 stitches remain.

Row 2: Rib.

Repeat rows 1 and 2 until 18 stitches remain.

Next 2 rows: Rib.

Bind off loosely in rib.

FINISHING

Fold piece in half and sew side and sleeve seams using mattress stitch.

EDGING

Using crochet hook and Sakura, work one round of single crochet (see p. 155) around neck opening, sleeve edges, and sweater bottom. Weave in ends and trim.

jeans

Using size 6 double-pointed needles and Tennessee, cast on 50 stitches for waist and distribute stitches as follows:

Needles 1 and 2: 15 stitches.

Needle 3: 20 stitches.

Place marker and join, making sure stitches aren't twisted. Work in the round as follows: Work 2 rounds in k1, p1 rib. Then knit every round until piece measures 2 inches from the beginning.

Divide for legs:

Knit 25 stitches and place on a stitch holder. Redistribute the remaining 25 stitches as follows:

Needles 1 and 2: 10 stitches.

Needle 3: 5 stitches.

Continue knitting every round until leg measures 6½ inches from the beginning. Purl one round. Bind off loosely.

Working on stitches on holder, reattach yarn and repeat as for the first leg.

FINISHING

With a length of Brilliant threaded into a yarn needle, embroider three spider web circles (see p. 156) on one side of the jeans using the photograph as a guide. Weave in all ends and trim.

> NOTE • You may choose to machine wash the jeans at this time to remove excess dye; this might cause them to slightly shrink in length, but will not affect the overall item. The sample is unwashed.

parasol

NOTE • This piece is worked in alternating colors of Rowan Summer Tweed, with unused color carried along on wrong side. Work colors throughout as follows: 2 rounds Brilliant, (1 round Bouquet, 1 round Brilliant), repeat to end.

TOP

With crochet hook and Brilliant, chain 4 and join with slip stitch to form a ring.

Round 1: Chain 1, 6 single crochet into the center of the ring, join with slip stitch.

Round 2: Chain 1, (single crochet once in next stitch, single crochet twice in the following stitch), repeat to the end of the round, join with slip stitch. (9 single crochet.)

Round 3: Chain 1, (single crochet once in next 2 stitches, single crochet twice in next stitch), repeat to the end of the round, join with slip stitch. (12 single crochet.)

Round 4: Chain 1, (single crochet once in the next 3 stitches, single crochet twice in the following stitch), repeat to the end of the round, join with slip stitch. (15 single crochet.)

Round 5: Chain 1, (single crochet once in the next 4 stitches, single crochet twice in next stitch) repeat to the end of the round, join with slip stitch. (18 single crochet.)

Round 6: Chain 1, (single crochet once in the next 5 stitches, single crochet twice in next stitch), repeat to the end of the round, join with slip stitch. (21 single crochet.)

Round 7: Chain 1, (single crochet once in the next 6 stitches, single crochet twice in next stitch), repeat to the end of the round, join with slip stitch. (24 single crochet.)

Round 8: Chain 1, (single crochet once in the next 7 stitches, single crochet twice in next stitch), repeat to the end of the round, join with slip stitch. (27 single crochet.)

Round 9: Chain 1, (single crochet once in the next 8 stitches, single crochet twice in next

skirt

Using size 6 double-pointed needles and Sakura, cast on 50 stitches for the waist and distribute stitches as follows:

Needles 1 and 2: 20 stitches.

Needle 3: 10 stitches.

Place a marker and join, making sure stitches aren't twisted. Knit in the round in k1, p1 rib for 3 rounds.

Knit every round until skirt measures 4 inches from the beginning. Purl 1 round.

RUFFLE

Round 1: kfb of every stitch. (100 stitches.)

Rounds 2 and 3: Knit.

Round 4: Purl.

Bind off loosely.

stitch), repeat to the end of the round, join with slip stitch. (30 single crochet.)

PICOT EDGING

With Sakura, crochet 1 round as follows: Chain 3, slip stitch in the same stitch, single crochet once in next stitch, slip stitch in next stitch. Repeat to the end of the round, join with slip stitch, and break yarn.

BOTTOM

Work as for top, through round 6 only and using only Bouquet.

HANDLE

Using two size 3 double-pointed needles and Tennessee, cast on 3 stitches. Make I-cord for 8 inches. Bind off and cut yarn, leaving a long tail. Wrap the tail tightly around 5 inches of the I-cord, shaping it into a hook as you wrap. Pull the unwrapped end through the center of the top and knot. Whipstitch knotted end down to secure and form a ball.

FINISHING

Push handle through the center of the bottom parasol piece. Holding the bottom and top pieces wrong sides together, lightly stuff the top with fiberfill and whipstitch the two pieces together using yarn threaded into a yarn needle. Tie the ribbon around the hook of the handle.

finials (make 2)

Using crochet hook and Bouquet, work as for the top through round 5. Change to Sakura and make a picot edging as for the top of the parasol. Break yarn.

Using crochet hook and Brilliant, work as for the top through round 2. Break yarn.

Sew smaller circle onto larger circle with yarn threaded into a yarn needle, using a whipstitch.

Repeat for the second finial, using Brilliant for the larger circle and Bouquet for the smaller circle.

putting it all together

Make a 1-inch ring on both ends of the flexible wire by winding the ends around the circle to hold it in place. With yarn threaded into a yarn needle, sew each wire circle to the back of one finial, and take extra stitches to create a loop for hanging the clothesline. Using two miniclothespins for each item, hang the parasol in the middle of the wire and hang the rest of the clothes, evenly spaced.

peas and carrots

I love this veggie combination, whether for dinner or for big, plush, fun pillows! My girls have been playing nonstop with the extra carrots I made, which make great fingers with which to point. The pillows are just as yummy with or without the feathers, which can be added later when your child is older.

yarn

- Peas: Crystal Palace Cotton Chenille (100% cotton; 98 yards/50 grams), 4 skeins in Cypress #4043; 2 skeins each in Limeade #1240 and Fern #2342
- Carrots: Crystal Palace Cotton Chenille, 3 skeins in Russet #403; 1 skein or leftover oddments from the peas, in Fern #2342

tools

- U.S. size 9 16-inch circular needle or size needed to obtain gauge
- U.S. size 9 set of four double-pointed needles or size needed to obtain gauge
- Bag of polyester fiberfill
- Green feather boa, at least 24 inches long (optional)
- Green thread (optional)
- Sewing needle (optional)
- Stitch markers
- Yarn needle
- Scissors
- Ruler or tape measure

gauge

4 stitches per inch with two strands held together

finished measurements

Carrots • 16, 14, and 11, and two at 10 inches

Peas in a pod • 20½ inches

pea pillow

POD

> NOTE • You will need to stuff the pod as you knit. Begin stuffing when the piece measures 6 inches from the beginning and stuff approximately every few inches as follows: create a trough in the center of the middle section for the peas to sit in, with a thinner layer of stuffing added along the bottom of the pod as you are building up the sides. Stuffing should be fairly compact but still squishy.

With size 9 double-pointed needles and two strands of Cypress held together, cast on 6 stitches placing 2 stitches each on three needles. Place a marker and join, making sure the stitches aren't twisted.

Rounds 1–5: Knit.

Round 6:

Needles 1 and 2: kfb, k1. 3 stitches on each needle.

Needle 3: kfb in both stitches. 4 stitches. 10 stitches total.

Rounds 7–9: Knit.

Round 10: kfb in every stitch.

Needles 1 and 2: 6 stitches.

Needle 3: 8 stitches. 20 stitches total.

Rounds 11–13: Knit.

Round 14: (k1, kfb), repeat to the end of the round.

Needles 1 and 2: 9 stitches.

Needle 3: 12 stitches. 30 stitches total.

Rounds 15–17: Knit.

Round 18: (k2, kfb), repeat to the end of the round.

Needles 1 and 2: 12 stitches.

Needle 3: 16 stitches. 40 stitches total.

Round 19: Knit.

Round 20: (k3, kfb), repeat to the end of the round.

Needles 1 and 2: 15 stitches.

Needle 3: 20 stitches. 50 stitches total.

Rounds 21 and 22: Knit.

Round 23: (k4, kfb), repeat to the end of the round.

Needles 1 and 2: 18 stitches.

Needle 3: 24 stitches. 60 stitches total.

Rounds 24 and 25: Knit.

Round 26: (k5, kfb), repeat to end of the round.

Needles 1 and 2: 21 stitches.

Needle 3: 28 stitches. 70 stitches total.

Next rounds: Change to circular needle and knit evenly until piece measures 18 inches from the beginning.

Round 1: (k5, k2tog), repeat to the end of the round. 60 stitches total remain.

Rounds 2 and 3: Knit.

Round 4: (k4, k2tog), repeat to the end of the round. 50 stitches total remain.

Rounds 5 and 6: Knit.

Round 7: Change to double-pointed needles and (k3, k2tog), repeat to the end of the round as follows:

Needles 1 and 2: 12 stitches.

Needle 3: 16 stitches. 40 stitches total remain.

Round 8: Knit.

Round 9: (k2, k2tog), repeat to the end of the round.

Needles 1 and 2: 9 stitches.

Needle 3: 12 stitches. 30 stitches total remain.

Rounds 10–12: Knit.

Round 13: (k1, k2tog), repeat to the end of the round.

Needles 1 and 2: 6 stitches. Needle 3: 8 stitches. 20 stitches total remain.

Rounds 14–16: Knit.

Round 17: k2tog, repeat to the end of the round.

Needles 1 and 2: 3 stitches.

Needle 3: 4 stitches. 10 stitches total remain.

Rounds 18–20: Knit.
Round 21:
Needles 1 and 2: k2tog, k1. 2 stitches on each needle.
Needle 3: k2tog, k2tog. (2 stitches.) 6 stitches total remain.
Rounds 22–26: Knit.

FINISHING

Finish stuffing. Cut yarn, leaving a long tail and thread into a yarn needle. Insert needle through remaining stitches, removing them from the needle. Pull tightly to close end and secure by invisibly weaving end into work. With yarn tail left from the cast-on, repeat to close other end of pod.

PEAS (make 3)

The individual peas are knitted in a stripe pattern with two strands of yarn held together.

STRIPE PATTERN

2 rounds Fern
2 rounds Limeade
Repeat.

With double-pointed needles and two strands of Fern held together, cast on 10 stitches and distribute on needles as follows:
Needles 1 and 2: 3 stitches.
Needle 3: 4 stitches.
Place a stitch marker and join, making sure stitches aren't twisted.
Round 1: Knit.
Round 2: kfb in every stitch.
Needles 1 and 2: 6 stitches.
Needle 3: 8 stitches. 20 stitches total.
Round 3: Knit.
Round 4: (k1, kfb), repeat to the end of the round.
Needles 1 and 2: 9 stitches.
Needle 3: 12 stitches. 30 stitches total.
Round 5: Knit.
Round 6: (k2, kfb), repeat to the end of the round.
Needles 1 and 2: 12 stitches.
Needle 3: 16 stitches. 40 stitches total.

Round 7: Knit.
Round 8: (k3, kfb), repeat to the end of the round.
Needles 1 and 2: 15 stitches.
Needle 3: 20 stitches. 50 stitches total.
Next rounds: Knit evenly for 12 rounds.

DECREASE ROUNDS

Round 1: (k3, k2tog), repeat to the end of the round. 40 stitches remain.
Round 2: Knit.
Round 3: (k2, k2tog), repeat to the end of the round. 30 stitches remain.
Round 4: Knit.
Round 5: (k1, k2tog), repeat to the end of the round. 20 stitches remain.
Round 6: Knit.
With the tail left from the cast-on, close the end with a few stitches. Stuff with fiberfill so it is firm but squishy.
Round 7: k2tog to the end of the round. 10 stitches remain.
Round 8: Knit.
Cut the yarn, leaving a long tail, and thread into a yarn needle. Insert needle through the remaining stitches, removing them from the double-pointed needles. Pull tightly to close the end, making sure it is properly stuffed. Secure by invisibly weaving end into the inside of the pea.

FINISHING

With a length of Cypress threaded into a yarn needle, attach the peas to the center trough of the pod. Hold the first pea in the desired position, and take a stitch in the bottom of it to anchor yarn. Pull the yarn all the way through the trough side of the pod and out the back. Insert the needle back into the pod about ¼ of an inch away from previous stitch. Pull the yarn back up to the pea and stitch through pod side of pea. Repeat this three times more. These stitches will secure the pea and create a tufting effect on the back of the pod.
Secure the yarn on the bottom of the pod by invisibly weaving the ends to the inside of the pod and trim.

Optional: Cut a 12-inch length of feather boa. With matching thread and sewing needle, sew the ends together to form a loop. Sew the joined ends onto one end of the pod.

carrots (make 5)

> NOTE • You will need to stuff the carrot every few inches as you knit.

With double-pointed needles and two strands of Russet held together, cast on 6 stitches and distribute 2 stitches on each of three needles. Place a marker and join, making sure stitches aren't twisted.

Rounds 1–6: Knit.

Round 7:
Needles 1 and 2: kfb, k1. 3 stitches per needle.
Needle 3: kfb, kfb. (4 stitches.) 10 stitches total.

Rounds 8–19: Knit.

Round 20:
Needles 1 and 2: kfb, k1, kfb. 5 stitches per needle.
Needle 3: kfb, k2, kfb. (6 stitches.) 16 stitches total.

Rounds 21–32: Knit.

Round 33:
Needles 1 and 2: kfb, k3, kfb. 7 stitches per needle.
Needle 3: kfb, k4, kfb. (8 stitches.) 22 stitches total.

Next rounds: Knit evenly to desired length (one each 16, 14, and 11 inches, and two measuring 10 inches from the beginning).

DECREASE ROUNDS

Round 1:
Needles 1 and 2: ssk, k2, k2tog. 5 stitches per needle remain.
Needle 3: ssk, k4, k2tog. 6 stitches remain. 16 stitches total.

Round 2: Knit.

Round 3:
Needles 1 and 2: ssk, k1, k2tog. 3 stitches per needle remain.
Needle 3: ssk, k2, k2tog. 4 stitches remain. 10 stitches total.

Round 4:
Needles 1 and 2: ssk, k1. 2 stitches per needle remain.
Needle 3: ssk, k2tog. 2 stitches remain. 6 stitches total.

FINISHING

Finish stuffing the carrot, making sure it is firm but still squishy. Cut the yarn, leaving a long tail, and thread it into a yarn needle. Insert needle through remaining stitches, removing them from double-pointed needles, and pull tightly to close end. Secure by taking a couple of small stitches and invisibly weaving in end, pulling the end through to the inside of the carrot. Trim.

STEMS (make 5)

Using two double-pointed needles as straight needles and two strands of Fern held together, cast on 2 stitches. Make I-cord for 12 inches. Bind off. Repeat 4 times. Sew one I-cord to the gathered top of each carrot. Braid three of the I-cords together tightly. Using a length of yarn threaded into a yarn needle, sew the braided I-cords together 2 inches from the end by drawing the needle through all of the I-cords. Wrap one I-cord around the braided stem, and with yarn and yarn needle, secure by taking a few stitches through the braid and the wrapped I-cord at both the top and bottom of the stem. Make a loop by sewing the top of the stem to the bottom of the stem. This creates a carrying handle.

Optional: Cut a 12-inch piece of feather boa. Loop it in half and sew the ends together with matching thread and sewing needle. Sew the joined end to the top of the bunch of carrots.

on the go, baby!

Who doesn't love a baby on the go? I know I do. I live on the go, and with four kids, I always feel like I have my own entourage! I know from experience that you need to take certain necessities along when you go out and about with your baby; how about a fun pacifier clip, handknit in cotton for easy care? Forget those manufactured numbers, they are never as sweet. You have three great pacifier clip designs here to choose from. I also included a fantastic felted bag for mom, designed to be ultrafunctional and hold every baby goodie in its own spot, but also to be pretty enough to carry forever!

Every little girl needs a pink sequined mini-tote—check out how I got those sequins knitted into the cabled cuff! Babies need to be cozy at all times, so I included a delicious and sweet cupcake hat, scarf, and mitten set that is sure to warm your heart as well as your baby. The other hat is called Frenchie, and utilizes a wrapping embroidery technique that I hope will become one of your favorites.

I always tell my kids to "move it and shake it" as we are on our way out the door. You can borrow my line whenever you'd like, but let me warn you, it doesn't always work to speed things along!

pacifier clips

For some reason, my babies were never too keen on pacifiers, so they have never been something to which I paid much attention. Lately, however, I have been seeing that not only do a lot of babies love their pacifiers, but their moms have clipped them right onto their shirts. How smart! These manufactured clips are not all that interesting, so I thought about making cuter ones. This collection of three clips turned out so sweet; the elephant, frog, and flower are great options for any baby, and I think you'll want to make all three. And they make fantastic baby gifts because they are small and knit up quickly. Pacifiers rule!

yarn

- Elephant: Rowan Handknit Cotton (100% cotton; 93 yards/50 grams), 1 skein each in Chime #204 and Bermuda #324
- Flower: Rowan Handknit Cotton, 1 skein each in Sugar #303, Gooseberry #219, and Mango Fool #319
- Frog: Rowan Handknit Cotton, 1 skein each in Gooseberry #219, Mango Fool #319, Celery #309, Bermuda #324, and Seafarer #318

tools

- U.S. size 3 set of four double-pointed needles or size needed to obtain gauge
- U.S. size E crochet hook
- Three purchased pacifier clips (remove any attached ribbon—leave only the plastic parts)
- Oddments of black embroidery floss
- Small bag of polyester fiberfill
- Stitch markers
- Scissors
- Yarn needle
- Ruler or tape measure

gauge

- 6 stitches per inch

flower

PETALS (make 5)

Using two double-pointed needles as straight needles and Sugar, cast on 10 stitches.

Rows 1–12: (k1, sl1 as if to purl), repeat to end of row. Cut yarn, leaving a 6-inch tail and thread into a yarn needle. Take the two needles out of the work, form the piece into a tube by gently squeezing. With a yarn needle, thread the tail through the live stitches. Turn inside out so knit side is facing you. Pull the tail through tightly to gather up the stitches, and secure.

Using crochet hook and Mango Fool, single crochet around outside edge of the petal, join with slip stitch. Cut the yarn and invisibly weave in the end on the inside of the petal.

Sew the five petals together at the gathered ends with several small stitches to create the flower.

CENTER

Using double-pointed needles and Mango Fool, cast on 6 stitches and distribute evenly, 2 stitches per needle. Place a stitch marker and join, making sure the stitches aren't twisted.

Round 1: Knit.

Round 2: On each needle, k1, m1, k1. 3 stitches per needle. 9 stitches total.

Rounds 3–5: Knit.

Round 6: On each needle, ssk, k1. 2 stitches per needle remain. 6 stitches total.

Round 7: Knit.

Cut yarn, leaving a long tail, and thread into a yarn needle. Insert needle through the live stitches, removing them from the double-pointed needles. Stuff with fiberfill. Pull tail tightly to close and sew to the center of the petals using a whipstitch.

Using two double-pointed needles as straight needles and Gooseberry, cast on 4 stitches. Work in garter stitch until piece measures 2½ inches.

Next row: ssk, k2. 3 stitches remain. Work I-cord for 4 inches. Bind off.

Using two double-pointed needles as straight needles and Gooseberry, cast on 5 stitches.

Row 1: k2, yo, k2tog, k1. (5 stitches.)

Row 2: Purl.

Rows 3 and 4: Repeat rows 1 and 2.

Row 5: ssk, yo, k2tog , k1. 4 stitches remain.

Row 6: p2tog, p2tog, pass second stitch over first stitch, cut yarn, and pull through remaining stitch. Invisibly weave in end on the back of the leaf. Thread yarn tail from cast-on into a yarn needle, insert needle through cast-on stitches, and pull tightly to gather.

Pull the garter stitch end of the stem through the hole in the pacifier holder and sew down securely with a whipstitch. Sew the flower to the stem just above where the garter stitch changes to I-cord (about 2 inches from the pacifier holder). Sew leaves to both sides of the I-cord stem. Pull the I-cord end of the stem through the clip and sew securely with a whipstitch.

elephant

Using 3 double-pointed needles and Chime, cast on 9 stitches and distribute 3 stitches on each of three needles. Place a stitch marker and join, making sure the stitches aren't twisted.

Round 1: Knit.

Round 2: On each needle, k1, m1, k1, m1, k1. 5 stitches per needle. 15 stitches total.

Round 3: Knit.

Round 4: On each needle, k1, m1, k3, m1, k1. 7 stitches per needle. 21 stitches total.

Rounds 5–7: Knit.

Round 8: On each needle, k1, k2tog, k1, k2tog, k1. 5 stitches per needle remain. 15 stitches total.

Rounds 9 and 10: Knit.

Round 11: On each needle, ssk, k1, k2tog. 3 stitches per needle remain. 9 stitches total. Close up the bottom hole with the tail left from the cast-on threaded through a yarn needle. Stuff the head with fiberfill until firm.

trunk

Rounds 12–17: Knit.

Round 18: On each needle, ssk, k1. 2 stitches per needle remain. 6 stitches total.

Rounds 19–28: Knit.

Stuff the head with fiberfill.

Round 29: k2tog across each needle, moving the 3 remaining stitches onto one needle. Using two double-pointed needles as straight needles, make I-cord for the trunk until it measures 4 inches. Bind off. Cut yarn, leaving an 8-inch tail, and pull tail through remaining stitch to secure.

Using two double-pointed needles as straight needles and Bermuda, cast on 4 stitches. Work in garter stitch until piece measures 2 inches. Bind off and cut yarn, leaving a 6-inch tail. Thread tail into a yarn needle, and pull the bound-off edge through the hole in the pacifier holder. Sew the bound-off end, using the whipstitch, to the back of the strap. Thread the tail from the cast-on edge into a yarn needle and sew the cast-on edge of the strap to the back of the elephant's head, using the whipstitch.

EARS (make 2)

Using the crochet hook and Chime, chain 4 stitches and join with slip stitch to make a ring.
Round 1: Single crochet 6 times into the center of the ring, join with slip stitch.
Round 2: Chain 1 stitch (single crochet once in the next stitch, single crochet twice in the following stitch), repeat to the end of the round, join with slip stitch. (9 single crochet.)
Round 3: Chain 1 stitch (single crochet once in the next 2 stitches, single crochet twice in the following stitch), repeat to the end of the round, join with slip stitch. (12 single crochet.)

Change to Bermuda.

Round 4: Chain 1 stitch (single crochet once in the next 3 stitches, single crochet twice in the following stitch), repeat to the end of the round, join with slip stitch. (15 single crochet.)
Cut yarn and pull tail through the remaining stitch to secure.

Using yarn tail threaded into a yarn needle, sew one ear to each side of the head using the whipstitch. Invisibly weave in ends and trim.

FINISHING

Pull trunk through the pacifier clip and securely sew the end of the trunk down with a whipstitch. With black embroidery floss and yarn needle, embroider two eyes and a mouth, making small, straight stitches. Pull the end of the embroidery floss through to the inside of the head and then out again firmly. Cut the floss so the end retracts back inside of the head.

frog

HEAD

Using four double-pointed needles and Gooseberry, cast on 9 stitches and distribute evenly, 3 stitches per needle. Place a stitch marker and join, making sure stitches aren't twisted.
Round 1: Knit.
Round 2: On each needle, k1, m1, k1, m1, k1. 5 stitches per needle. 15 stitches total.
Rounds 3–6: Knit.
Round 7: On each needle, ssk, k1, k2tog. 3 stitches per needle remain. 9 stitches total.
Round 8: Knit.

Stuff with fiberfill. Cut yarn, leaving a 6-inch tail, and thread it into a yarn needle. Insert needle through the live stitches, removing them from the double-pointed needles. Pull tightly to gather and stitch to secure. Do not trim tail.

EYES (make 2)

Using two double-pointed needles as straight needles and Gooseberry, loosely cast on 1 stitch, leaving a 1-inch tail.
Row 1: Knit into the front, back, and front again of the stitch. (3 stitches.)
Row 2: Knit.
Row 3: Purl.
Row 4: Knit, do not turn. One stitch at a time, pass the second and third stitches over the first stitch. Cut the yarn and pull the tail through the remaining stitch. Stuff the eye with the cast-on yarn tail. Gather up with the other tail on a yarn needle to create a bobble. Sew to the head with whipstitch.

BODY

Using four double-pointed needles and Gooseberry, cast on 9 stitches and distribute evenly, 3 stitches per needle. Place a stitch marker and join, making sure stitches aren't twisted.
Round 1: Knit.

Round 2: On each needle, k1, m1, k1, m1, k1.
5 stitches per needle. 15 stitches total.
Round 3: Knit.
Round 4: On each needle, k1, m1, k3, m1, k1.
7 stitches per needle. 21 stitches total.
Rounds 5–8: Knit.
Round 9: On each needle, ssk, k3, k2tog.
5 stitches per needle remain. 15 stitches total.
Round 10: Knit.
Round 11: On each needle, ssk, k1, k2tog.
3 stitches per needle remain. 9 stitches total.
Round 12: Knit.
Cut yarn, leaving a 6-inch tail, and thread into
a yarn needle. Insert needle through the live
stitches, removing them from the double-pointed
needles. Stuff with fiberfill. Pull yarn tightly and
stitch to secure.

LEGS AND ARMS (make 4)

Using two double-pointed needles as straight
needles and Gooseberry, cast on 2 stitches.
Make I-cord for 1½ inches. Bind off.

HANDS AND FEET (make 4)

Using two double-pointed needles as straight
needles and Gooseberry, *loosely* cast on 1 stitch,
leaving a 2-inch tail.
Row 1: Knit into the front and back of the stitch
until 5 stitches are on the needle.
Row 2: Knit.
Row 3: Purl.
Row 4: Knit, do not turn. One stitch at a time,
pass the second, third, fourth, and fifth stitches
over the first stitch to create a bobble.
Cut the yarn, leaving a 6-inch tail, and thread into
a yarn needle. Stuff the bobble with the 2-inch
cast-on tail. Gather up the edges and stitch to
secure into a ball. Repeat three times. Sew one
bobble to the end of each arm and leg.

FINISHING

Using the photograph as a guide, and whipstitch,
sew the head to the center top of the body. Sew
the arms to where the head meets the body. Sew
the legs to the bottom of the body. With black
embroidery floss threaded into a yarn needle and

satin stitch, embroider a V-shaped mouth and
two small eyes.

STRAP

Using two double-pointed needles as straight
needles and Bermuda, cast on 4 stitches. Work
in garter stitch until piece measures 6½ inches.
Bind off.

LEAVES (make 3)

Using two double-pointed needles as straight
needles and Celery, cast on 5 stitches.
Row 1: k2, yo, k2tog, k1. (5 stitches.)
Row 2: Purl.
Rows 3 and 4: Repeat rows 1 and 2.
Row 5: ssk, yo, k2tog, k1. 4 stitches remain.
Row 6: p2tog, p2tog, pass the second stitch over
the first stitch, cut the yarn, and pull it through
remaining stitch. Invisibly weave in the end on
the back of the leaf. Thread the cast-on tail into
a yarn needle and stitch through the cast-on
stitches. Pull the yarn tightly to gather, and
secure. Sew the leaves to the bottom of the frog
so that they fan out.

STEM

Using two double-pointed needles as straight
needles and Celery, cast on 2 stitches. Make
I-cord for 5 inches. Bind off.

BUTTERFLY

body • Using two double-pointed needles as
straight needles and Seafarer, cast on 2 stitches.
Make I-cord for 1 inch.
Next row: kfb, kfb. (4 stitches.)
Cut the yarn, leaving a tail, and thread it into a
yarn needle. Insert needle into the live stitches,
removing them from the double-pointed needle.
Pull tightly to gather, and stitch to secure.

wings (make 2) • Using two double-pointed
needles as straight needles and Mango Fool,
cast on 3 stitches.
Row 1: kfb, k2. (4 stitches.)
Row 2: k3, kfb. (5 stitches.)
Row 3: Knit.

Row 4: Bind off 2, k2. 3 stitches remain.

Row 5: k3, cast on 2. (5 stitches.)

Row 6: Knit.

Row 7: k3, k2tog. 4 stitches remain.

Row 8: ssk, k2. 3 stitches remain.

Bind off. Cut yarn, leaving a tail, and thread into a yarn needle. Insert needle through the last stitch to secure. Sew wing to one side of the butterfly body. Repeat for the second wing.

Pull one end of the strap through the pacifier holder and one end through the clip. Sew down securely, using the whipstitch on the back side of the strap. Using the photograph as a guide, sew the frog to the strap about 1 inch from the clip so that it leans back slightly. Sew stem to the strap so it forms a loop. Sew the butterfly to the bottom of the stem about ½ inch from the pacifier holder.

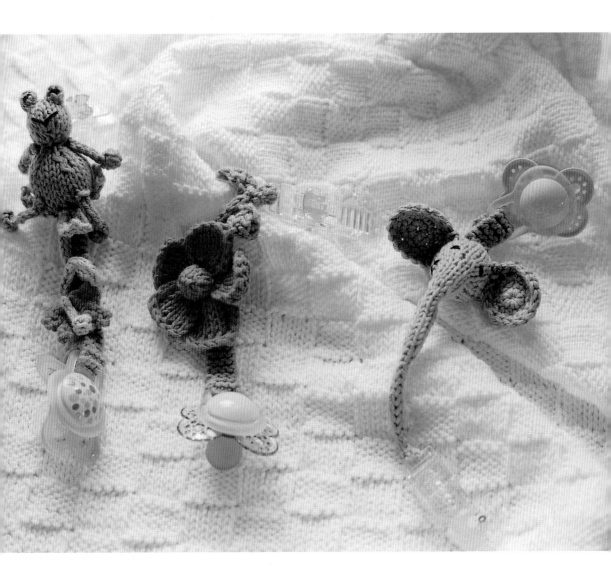

fruit loops bag

When I had my first baby, I got all of the equipment you could imagine. Of course, I also got a big, huge, ugly diaper bag. It was red (shudder). It makes me laugh when I think about it—why do you need such an enormous bag? I have never figured it out. By the time I had my fourth child, I was throwing a diaper, and a Baggie of wipes into my purse on my way out the door!

This felted project is the antidote to bad diaper bags. I designed Fruit Loops to be fun and practical, with a bottle pocket on the outside for easy access, a large pocket on the inside for a thin wipe holder, and an interior loop for a pacifier clip. There is room inside for a few diapers, a toy or book, and a snack. That's all you need. And long after the need for a diaper bag passes, the bottle pocket could hold your cell phone, the inside pocket your wallet, the loop your knitting needles or keys. There will be plenty of room for your knitting project as well. Think to the future and make a bag with staying power that looks good, too!

yarn

- Cascade 220 (100% Peruvian highland wool; 220 yards/100 grams), 5 skeins in Black #8555 (used doubled throughout); 1 skein each or oddments (see note) of Purple Hyacinth #7808, Lagoon #7812, Robin's Egg Blue #8905, Orange #7824, Persimmon #9466, Coral #7830, Pink #4192, Lime Green #8910, and Magenta #7803

tools

- U.S. size 11 24-inch circular needle or size needed to obtain gauge
- U.S. size 11 set of two double-pointed needles (optional)
- Stitch markers
- Three stitch holders
- Mesh lingerie bag
- Scissors
- Yarn needle
- Ruler or tape measure

gauge

- 3 stitches per inch with two strands held together

finished measurements after felting

- Length: 11 inches
- Width: 5¼ inches
- Height: 9 inches
- These measurements will vary slightly due to the felting process.

NOTE • You could embroider the loops with only one or two colors, or look through your stash for any colorful wool that will felt. You only need a small amount of any one color. Also, I made the Rosebud hat from *Itty-Bitty Hats* to match the bag using the leftover yarn. This makes a cute gift set!

With the 24-inch circular needle and two strands of Black held together, cast on 40 stitches. Work in garter stitch for 40 rows. Do not bind off.

Knit 1 row across the base. Turn the corner on the base and pick up 20 stitches (1 stitch in each ridge) along the edge. Turn the corner again and pick up 40 stitches. Turn the corner again and pick up 20 stitches. 120 stitches total.

Place a marker for the beginning of the round and join.

Rounds 1–10: Knit.

Round 11: k6, bind off 2 stitches, k62, bind off 2 stitches, knit to the end. 116 stitches remain.

Round 12: k6, cast on 2 stitches, k62, cast on 2 stitches, knit to the end. (120 stitches.)

Rounds 13–28: Knit.

Round 29: k27, bind off 2 stitches, k46, bind off 2 stitches, knit to the end. 116 stitches remain.

Round 30: k27, cast on 2 stitches, k46, cast on 2 stitches, knit to the end. (120 stitches.)

Rounds 31–38: Knit.

Round 39: k23, bind off 2 stitches, k55, bind off 2 stitches, knit to the end. (116 stitches.)

Round 40: k23, cast on 2 stitches, k55, cast on 2 stitches, knit to the end. (120 stitches.)

Rounds 41–49: Knit.

Round 50: k40, (k3, k2tog) four times, k40, (k3, k2tog) four times. 112 stitches remain.

Start the loop pattern for the top of the bag as follows:

Round 51: (bind off 2 stitches, k4), repeat to the end of the round. There will be 2 bound-off stitches followed by 5 knit stitches across the round.

Round 52: (cast on 2 stitches, k5), repeat to the end of the round.

Rounds 53–55: Knit.

Round 56: (k3, bind off 2 stitches, k1), repeat to the end of the round. There will be 2 bound-off stitches followed by 5 knit stitches.

Round 57: (k3, cast on 2 stitches, k2), repeat to the end of the round.

Rounds 58–60: Knit.

Rounds 61 and 62: Repeat rounds 51 and 52.

Rounds 63–66: Knit.

Bind off for the handles as follows:
Knit 10 stitches, bind off the next 20 stitches, knit 9 more stitches, and place the last 10 stitches on the first stitch holder. Bind off the next 16 stitches, knit 9 more stitches, and place the last 10 stitches on the second stitch holder. Bind off 20 stitches, knit 9 more stitches, and place the last 10 stitches on a third stitch holder. Bind off the remaining 16 stitches.

You may want to use two double-pointed needles in the same size as the circular needle to knit the handles back and forth. It is faster and less cumbersome. If not, continue with the circular needle.

Work back and forth on the first 10 stitches that remain on the needle as follows:

Row 1: Knit.

Row 2: k1, p8, k1.

Repeat rows 1 and 2 until the handle measures 36 inches. Use kitchener stitch (see p. 151) to graft the handle to the stitches on the first holder. Repeat by placing the stitches from the second holder on the needle and work rows 1 and 2 until handle measures 36 inches. Use kitchener stitch to graft the second handle to the stitches on the third holder.

With the circular needle and two strands of Black held together, cast on 20 stitches. Work in stockinette stitch for 10 inches, ending with a purl row.

Next row: (k3, k2tog), repeat to the end of the row. 16 stitches remain.

Bind off tightly. Sew three sides of the pocket to the side of the bag with a single strand of yarn threaded into a yarn needle, leaving the top open. The top of the pocket in the bound-off edge and is left open.

INSIDE POCKET

With the circular needle and two strands of Black held together, cast on 25 stitches. Work in stockinette stitch for 8 inches. Bind off all stitches. Sew to the inside on one side of the bag with a single strand of yarn threaded into a yarn needle.

PACIFIER LOOP

You could use double-pointed needles at this point for the I-cord, however, I simply slid the stitches back and forth on my circular needle. With two strands of Black held together, cast on 3 stitches. Make I-cord for 5 inches. Bind off all stitches. Create a loop with the cord and secure, using a yarn needle and a single strand of yarn, with a few stitches. Sew the loop to the inside of the bag, opposite the bottle pocket.

EMBROIDERY

Thread two strands held together of any of the colors of yarn into a yarn needle. Use the straight stitch (see p. 158) to form a ring around each hole. Repeat, alternating the colors on each hole. For the holes at the bottom of the bag, tighten up the hole a bit after you have embroidered it by running the yarn around the hole through the straight stitches and pulling tight. Weave in all ends and trim.

FELTING

Place the bag in the mesh lingerie bag and pour a small amount of gentle detergent over it. Run the bag through a hot wash cycle with a cold rinse, with the water level set at the lowest possible. I throw in an old T-shirt to add more agitation. Repeat until you can't see the individual knit stitches any longer. Make sure to check your bag after each washing and pull it into shape. It took me three wash cycles to felt this bag, but the number of cycles required will vary with each machine.

After it is felted, really pull and form the bag into the desired shape. If you wish, stuff it with plastic bags to hold its form. Let it air dry; this may take several days.

> NOTE • It is best whenever possible to use a top-loading washer for this process for better agitation and so you can stop the machine periodically to check on the bag's progress.

quick knit mini-tote

Little girls love sequins and they love pink. I wanted to figure out a way to combine the two in this ultraeasy tote without sewing each sequin on one by one. The answer was to purchase sequins that were threaded together from the craft-store ribbon section. I then ran the thread of sequins along with the yarn in the cable cuff at the top of the tote. The effect is great, and adds just enough sparkle to delight any glitz-loving girl! The 6-inch tote is the perfect size for a juice box and snack, tiny board book or two, or a knitted toy. And it took an hour or two at the most to knit!

yarn

- Blue Sky Alpacas Bulky (50% alpaca, 50% wool; 45 yards/100grams), 2 skeins in Peace Pink #1018

tools

- U.S. size 15 24-inch circular needle, or size needed to obtain gauge
- U.S. size 15 set of two double-pointed needles (optional)
- 4 yards of threaded sequins
- Cable needle (or one size 15 double-pointed needle)
- Straight pins
- Scissors
- Yarn needle
- Ruler or tape measure

gauge

- 2 stitches per inch
- finished size: 6 inches by 6 inches

BAG

With circular needle and Peace Pink, cast on 24 stitches. (K1, sl1 with yarn in back), repeat across this and every following row until the bag measures 6 inches. Remove the work from the circular needle, and gently form the bag into a tube. Place the separated stitches back on the circular needle and bind off. Cut the yarn and weave in the end with a yarn needle. Trim.

SEQUINED CABLE CUFF

With circular needle and Peace Pink, cast on 6 stitches. Carry and knit the threaded sequins along with the yarn for the middle 2 stitches *only* on rows 1 through 4 and the middle 4 stitches on row 5. When you aren't knitting with the sequins, drop that strand and knit only with Peace Pink, then pick it up and carry it with the yarn again when it is time to knit the specified stitches.

Row 1: Knit.

Row 2: k1, p4, k1.

Rows 3 and 4: Repeat rows 1 and 2.

Row 5 (cable row): k1, place 2 stitches on the cable needle and hold to the front, k2, k2 from cable needle, k1.

Repeat rows 2 through 5 until the cuff measures 12½ inches. Bind off all stitches. Cut the yarn, leaving a long tail, and pull it through the remaining stitch.

HANDLE

With two double-pointed needles or the circular needle and Peace Pink, cast on 4 stitches. Make I-cord for 12 inches. Bind off all stitches, cut the yarn, and pull it through the remaining stitch.

FINISHING

Pin the cuff around the top of the bag and whipstitch it in place along both the top and bottom cuff edges. Sew the handles to the inside of the bag, using the photograph as a guide.

cupcake baby set

I must have cupcakes on the brain! I absolutely love them in any form, and buy cupcake cookbooks and magazines just to find different ways to decorate the little cakes. For my daughter's seventh birthday party, we made cupcakes with candy fruit slices on top. They were a colorful hit, but you can never beat a white frosted cupcake with a cherry on top. That's why I designed this beautiful little set that's full of cupcake splendor. It is like the perfect classic cupcake, only you can wear it!

yarn

- RY Classic Cashsoft Baby DK (57% extra fine merino, 33% microfiber, 10% cashmere; 142 yards/50 grams), 1 skein each in Pixie #807 and Snowman #800
- RY Classic Cashsoft DK (57% extra fine merino, 33% microfiber, 10% cashmere; 142 yards/50 grams), 1 skein in Poppy #512
- Small amount of DK-weight brown yarn for the cherry stem on the hat (sample was worked in Rowan Handknit Cotton in Tope #253)

tools

- U.S. size 7 16-inch circular needle or size needed to obtain gauge
- U.S. size 7 set of four double-pointed needles or size needed to obtain gauge
- U.S. size 3 set of two double-pointed needles or size needed to obtain gauge
- U.S. size 7 straight or 24-inch circular needles, or size needed to obtain gauge
- U.S. size G crochet hook
- Small amount of polyester fiberfill
- Stitch marker
- Scissors
- Yarn needle
- Ruler or tape measure

gauge

- 5 stitches per inch on size 7 needles

hat

sizes

- newborn (3–6 months, 6–12 months, 1–2 years)

With the 16-inch circular needle and Pixie, cast on 64 (72, 80, 88) stitches. Work in k1, p1 rib until the hat measures 2½, (3, 3½, 4) inches. Switch to Snowman and purl 1 round. Knit every round in Snowman until the hat measures 4½ (5, 5½, 6) inches from the beginning. Begin the decrease sequence.

DECREASE ROUNDS

Round 1: (k6, k2tog), repeat to the end of the round. 56 (63, 70, 77) stitches remain.
Round 2: (k5, k2tog), repeat to the end of the round. 48 (54, 60, 66) stitches remain.
Round 3: Knit.
Round 4: Change to size 7 double-pointed needles, working onto them as follows:
Needle 1: (k4, k2tog), repeat 3 (3, 3, 4) times. 15 (15, 15, 20) stitches remain.
Needle 2: (k4, k2tog), repeat 3 (3, 3, 4) times. 15 (15, 15, 20) stitches remain.
Needle 3: (k4, k2tog), repeat 2 (3, 4, 3) times. 10 (15, 20, 15) stitches remain.
40 (45, 50, 55) total stitches remain. The fourth needle is now the working needle.
Round 5: (k3, k2tog), repeat to the end of the round. 32 (36, 40, 44) stitches remain. The next rounds create the point of the hat.
Rounds 6–8: Knit.

Round 9: (k2, k2tog), repeat to the end of the round. 24 (27, 30, 33), stitches remain.
Round 10: Knit.
Round 11: (k1, k2tog), repeat to the end of the round. 16 (18, 20, 22) stitches remain.
Round 12: k2tog, repeat to the end of the round. 8 (9, 10, 11) stitches remain.

Cut the yarn and thread into a yarn needle. Pull through the remaining live stitches. Gather up tight and stitch to secure. Turn the hat inside out so that the purl side is facing outward. This is now the right side of the hat. Weave the end to the inside and trim.

With the crochet hook and Snowman, and working into the first purled round of Snowman, complete one round of picot edging as follows: (Chain 3 stitches, slip stitch into the same stitch, single crochet once into the next stitch, slip stitch into the next stitch), repeat to the end of the round, join with slip stitch. Cut the yarn and weave the end into the inside of the hat. Trim.

CHERRY

With the crochet hook and Poppy, leave a 6-inch tail, chain 4 stitches and join them in a ring with a slip stitch. Work in the round as follows:
Round 1: Single crochet 6 times into the center of the ring, join with a slip stitch.
Round 2: (Single crochet twice into the next stitch, single crochet once in the following stitch), repeat to the end of the round, join with a slip stitch.
Rounds 3 and 4: Single crochet once in each of the stitches, join with a slip stitch.
Round 5 (decrease round): Single crochet once in every other stitch to the end of the round.

Stuff with fiberfill until the cherry is firm. Cut the yarn, leaving a 6-inch tail, and pull the end through the last stitch. Threat the tail into a yarn needle and gather up the end tightly. Weave end in and trim. Repeat on the other end of the cherry. Sew the cherry to the top of the hat using whipstitch.

STEM

With two size 3 double-pointed needles and brown, cast on 2 stitches. Make I-cord for 1½ inches. Knit the 2 stitches together, cut the yarn, and pull through the remaining stitch. Cut yarn and thread into a yarn needle. Sew the stem securely to the top of the cherry and give the stem a twist so it curls slightly. Weave in ends.

scarf

finished measurement

• 6 inches (slightly stretched) by 28 inches

With the size 7 straight needles or 24-inch circular needle used as straight needles and Snowman, cast on 30 stitches. Work in rib for the entire scarf as follows:
Row 1: (k2, p2), repeat to the end of the row.
Row 2: p2 (k2, p2), repeat to the end of the row. Repeat rows 1 and 2 and at the same time follow the stripe pattern.

STRIPE PATTERN

Rows 1–4: Snowman
Rows 4–8: Pixie
Work in rib and stripe pattern until the scarf measures 28 inches. Bind off all stitches in rib.

CHERRIES (make 6)

Make cherries as for the hat. Sew three cherries to each end of the scarf

mittens

size

• 0–6 months (6–12 months, 1–2 years)

With the four size 7 double-pointed needles and Pixie, cast on 22 (24, 26) stitches as follows:
Needle 1: 7 (8, 9) stitches.
Needle 2: 7 (8, 9) stitches.
Needle 3: 9 (9, 8) stitches.

Place a marker and join, making sure the stitches aren't twisted. Work in the round in k1, p1 rib until the mitten measures 1½ (1¾, 2) inches. Switch to Snowman and purl 1 round. Change to stockinette and knit every round in Snowman until the mitten measures 3 (3½, 4) inches from the beginning. Begin the decrease rounds.

DECREASE ROUNDS

Round 1: (k2, k2tog), repeat to the end of the round. 17 (18, 20) stitches remain.
Rounds 2 and 3: Knit.
Round 4: (k2, k2tog), repeat to the end of the round. For the smallest size only, knit the remaining stitch. 13 (14, 15) stitches remain.
Round 5: Knit.
Round 6: (k1 [0, 1] stitches, k2tog), repeat to the end of the round. 7 (7, 8) stitches remain.

Cut the yarn, thread tail into a yarn needle, and pull through the live stitches. Pull up tight and gather. Turn the mitten inside out. The purl side is the right side of the mitten. Weave in the ends to the wrong side of the mitten.

Repeat to make the second mitten.

PICOT EDGING

With Snowman and the crochet hook, make a picot edging around the mitten the same as for the hat.

CHERRY (make 2)

With two size 7 double-pointed needles used as straight needles and Poppy, cast on 1 stitch *loosely*, leaving a 2-inch tail.
Row 1: Knit into the front and back of the stitch until 5 stitches are on the right needle.
Row 2: Knit.
Row 3: Purl.
Row 4: Knit, do not turn, pass the second, third, fourth, and fifth stitches over the first stitch. Cut the yarn and thread into a yarn needle. Stuff the bobble with the tail from the cast-on. Stitch closed tightly, and sew to the tip of the mitten.

frenchie

I intended to give this hat as a gift to a friend having her second baby this summer, but after it was finished, I loved it so much that I just had to add it to this collection instead. I'll have to design another one for her later! The colors, stripes, and embroidery make a charming combination. In fact, as I was working on it, a woman walked by me and exclaimed, "My, that hat looks so French!" I agreed, thus the name.

size

- 0–6 months (6–12 months, 1–2 years, 2 years and up)

yarn

- GGH Samoa (50% cotton, 50% microfiber; 104 yds/50 grams), 1 skein each in White #18, Yellow #5, Light Blue #85, and Dark Blue #56

tools

- U.S. size 7 16-inch circular needle, or size needed to obtain gauge
- U.S size 7, set of four double-pointed needles or size needed to obtain gauge
- U.S. size G crochet hook
- Pom-pom tree or pom-pom maker
- Stitch marker
- Scissors
- Yarn needle
- Ruler or tape measure

gauge

- 5 stitches per inch

TIP • After you make this hat, use your leftover yarn to make Stars out of *Itty-Bitty Hats.* It uses the exact same yarn and colors.

NOTE • When making many color changes, I weave in the cut ends a few at a time as I go along. This saves you from having to do all of them at the end.

With circular needle and Light Blue, cast on 64 (72, 80, 88) stitches. Place a stitch marker and join, making sure the stitches aren't twisted. Knit every stitch until the hat measures 1½ inches. Begin the stripe and texture patterns.

STRIPE AND TEXTURE PATTERN

Rounds 1–4: Seed stitch (see p. 142) with White.
Rounds 5–11: Knit with Dark Blue.
Round 12: Purl with Yellow.
Round 13: Knit with Yellow.
Rounds 14 and 15: Repeat rounds 12 and 13.
Rounds 16 and 17: Knit with Light Blue.
Rounds 18–21: Seed stitch with White.
Change to the stripe pattern and work until the hat measures 5 (5½, 6, 6½) inches from the beginning.

STRIPE PATTERN

2 rounds Dark Blue
2 rounds Light Blue
Begin the decrease sequence, *at the same time* continuing the same stripe pattern through round 11.

DECREASE ROUNDS

Round 1: (k6, k2tog), repeat to the end of the round. 56 (63, 70, 77) stitches remain.
Round 2: (k5, k2tog), repeat to the end of the round. 48 (54, 60, 66) stitches remain.
Round 3: Knit.
Round 4: Change to the double-pointed needles and knit directly onto three of them as follows: Needle 1: (k4, k2tog), repeat 3 (3, 3, 4) times. 15 (15, 15, 20) stitches remain.

Needle 2: (k4, k2tog), repeat 3 (3, 3, 4) times. 15 (15, 15, 20) stitches remain.

Needle 3: (k4, k2tog), repeat 2 (3, 4, 3) times. 10 (15, 20, 15) stitches remain.

40 (45, 50, 55) total stitches remain.

The fourth needle is now the working needle.

Round 5: (k3, k2tog), repeat to the end of the round. 32 (36, 40, 44) stitches remain.

The next rounds create the point on top of the hat.

Rounds 6–10: Knit.

Round 11: (k2, k2tog), repeat to the end of the round. 24 (27, 30, 33) stitches remain.

Begin the new stripe pattern, *at the same time* continuing on with the decrease sequence.

STRIPE PATTERN

2 rounds in Dark Blue

2 rounds in Yellow

Repeat this stripe pattern through round 23.

Rounds 12–16: Knit.

Round 17: (k1, k2tog), repeat to the end of the round. 16 (18, 20, 22) stitches remain.

Rounds 18–22: Knit.

Round 23: k2tog, repeat to the end of the round. 8 (9, 10, 11) stitches remain.

Change to Yellow.

Rounds 24–28: Knit.

Round 29: k2tog, repeat to the end of the round. Knit any remaining stitches. 4 (5, 5, 6) stitches remain.

EMBROIDERY

In the 7 rounds of the Dark Blue section of the hat, start with White and the crochet hook, and chain stitch through the hat in a wave pattern (see p. 154). Take a long length of White, thread into a yarn needle, and tightly wrap the chain stitch (see p. 159). Repeat with Yellow, creating opposite waves.

TASSEL

Make a 1-inch tassel (see p. 153), holding strands of Light Blue and White together and wrapping 20 times (40 wraps total). Sew it to the top of the hat and take several stitches through the tassel to make it stand straight up.

playtime!

There is something so sweet about knitted toys. They are fun to handle, have a nice weight, and of course are made by thoughtful hands. Knitting them is at the top of my list, and I hope I can encourage you to join in. The toy projects offered throughout this book all make for wonderful knitting, but none more so than the Playtime collection. These are little projects, so you can complete them quickly—always a plus.

The Cupcake Tea Set is one of the best projects I have ever designed. It's a guaranteed winner, and kids of any age, and even some adults, will love to play with this gorgeous toy. The knitted sugar cubes, golden spoons, and sequin-filled tea bags all add to the fun. Cupcakes and tea for all!

The Dotted Chickens are so much fun you'll have to make more than one. The Three Pigs and a Wolf finger puppets will provide lots of fun interaction time for parents and children, plus those pigs are just plain cute on little fingers! There are three houses included for the pigs, a big black cooking pot, and a chimney for the wolf to climb through.

I love all of these lighthearted projects, and I hope you make Playtime a part of your daily schedule.

cupcake tea set

This is childhood fun at its finest! This twenty-five-piece set has it all, from sugar cubes to sequin-filled tea bags to golden spoons and everything in between. While I was knitting this set last summer at my neighborhood pool, I would often have a crowd of kids standing around me asking questions about what I was making. When I told them it was a knitted tea set, the kids got the biggest smiles on their faces. They loved it. The kids watching me put the spout on the teapot stared in disbelief. After I finished, my own girls, who are seven and ten years old, paraded their friends into my studio to steal a glimpse of the set, which was waiting to be photographed. They just couldn't wait to get their hands on it. I told them that as soon as it was returned from the photography studio, it would be fair game for play. I think this is the sign of a successful design for children, when their fingers are just itching to get ahold of it!

yarn

- Rowan Handknit Cotton (100% cotton; 93 yards/ 50 grams), 3 skeins each in Bleached #263 and Shell #310; 1 skein each in Sugar #303, Double Chocolate #315, and Rosso #215

- Sample spoons are knit in Rowan Lurex Shimmer (80% viscose, 20% polyester; 104 yards/25 grams), 1 skein in Antique White Gold #332. Suggested substitutes are Berroco Metallic FX (85% rayon, 15% metallic; 85 yards/25 grams), 1 skein in Silver #1002 or Tahki Yarns Star (60% nylon, 40% polyester; 163 yards/20 grams), 1 skein in #007

- Rowan Kidsilk Haze (70% super kid mohair, 30% silk; 229 yards/25 grams), 1 skein in Grace #580

tools

- U.S. size 3 16-inch circular needle, or size needed to obtain gauge
- U.S. size 3 set of five double-pointed needles, or size needed to obtain gauge
- U.S. size G crochet hook
- U.S. size D crochet hook
- U.S. size E crochet hook
- Four ½-inch flower stickers
- Five pipe cleaners
- Small bag of polyester fiberfill
- Small bag of polly-pellets
- Stitch marker

- Scissors
- Yarn needle
- Ruler or tape measure

gauge

- 6 stitches per inch on size 3 needles with Rowan Handknit Cotton

cake plate (make 2)

With four double-pointed needles and Bleached, cast on 60 stitches, 20 on each of 3 needles. Place a stitch marker and join, making sure the stitches aren't twisted. Continue as follows:
Round 1: Seed stitch (k1, p1), repeat to the end of the round.
Round 2: Seed stitch (p1, k1), repeat to the end of the round.
Rounds 3 and 4: Knit.
Round 5: (k3, k2tog), repeat to the end of the round. 16 stitches per needle remain. 48 stitches total.
Rounds 6 and 7: Knit.
Round 8: (k2, k2tog), repeat to the end of the round. 12 stitches per needle remain. 36 stitches total.
Rounds 9 and 10: Knit.

Round 11: k1, k2tog, repeat to the end of the round. 8 stitches per needle remain. 24 stitches total.

Round 12: k2tog, repeat to the end of the round. 4 stitches per needle remain. 12 stitches total.

Round 13: Knit.

Round 14: k2tog, repeat to the end of the round. 2 stitches per needle remain. 6 stitches total.

Cut the yarn and thread the tail into a yarn needle. Pull the tail through the remaining live stitches and pull up tight.

CROCHET EDGING

With the size E crochet hook and Sugar, single crochet one round on the outer edge of the plate.

With the crochet hook and Shell, make picot edging on the outer edge of the plate as follows: (Chain 3 stitches, slip stitch into the same stitch, single crochet once into the next stitch, slip stitch into the next stitch), repeat to the end of the round, join with a slip stitch.

saucers (make 2)

With four double-pointed needles and Bleached, cast on 50 stitches. Divide the stitches over three needles as follows:

Needles 1 and 2: 15 stitches.

Needle 3: 20 stitches.

Place a stitch marker and join, making sure the stitches aren't twisted.

Round 1: Seed stitch (k1, p1), repeat to the end of the round.

Round 2: Seed stitch (p1, k1), repeat to the end of the round.

Rounds 3 and 4: Knit.

Round 5: (k3, k2tog), repeat to the end of the round.

Needles 1 and 2: 12 stitches remain.

Needle 3: 16 stitches remain.

40 stitches total remain.

Rounds 6 and 7: Knit.

Round 8: (k2, k2tog), repeat to the end of the round.

Needles 1 and 2: 9 stitches remain.

Needle 3: 12 stitches remain.

30 stitches total remain.

Round 9: Knit.

Round 10: (k1, k2tog), repeat to the end of the round.

Needles 1 and 2: 6 stitches remain.

Needle 3: 8 stitches remain.

20 stitches total remain.

Round 11: Knit.

Round 12: k2tog, repeat to the end of the round.

Needles 1 and 2: 3 stitches remain.

Needle 3: 4 stitches remain.

10 stitches total remain.

Complete two rounds of crochet edging as for the cake plate.

serving plate (make 1)

With the 16-inch circular needle and Bleached, cast on 80 stitches. Place a stitch marker and join, making sure the stitches aren't twisted.

Round 1: Seed stitch (k1, p1), repeat to the end of the round.

Round 2: Seed stitch (p1, k1), repeat to the end of the round.

Rounds 3 and 4: Knit.

Round 5: (k6, k2tog), repeat to the end of the round. 70 stitches remain.

Rounds 6 and 7: Knit.

Round 8: (k5, k2tog), repeat to the end of the round. 60 stitches remain.

Rounds 9 and 10: Knit.

Change to three double-pointed needles on the next round, knitting directly onto them and distributing the stitches as follows:

Needles 1 and 2: 18 stitches.

Needle 3: 24 stitches.

The fourth needle is now your working needle.

Round 11: (k4, k2tog), repeat to the end of the round. 50 stitches remain.

Rounds 12 and 13: Knit.

For the remainder of the serving plate, complete rounds 5 through 11 from the saucer instructions and finish with two rounds of crochet edging.

mini-cupcakes (make 6)

Make two cupcake bases and two sides in each of the following colors: Sugar, Double Chocolate, and Shell.

BASE

With Sugar, Double Chocolate, or Shell and the size G crochet hook, chain 6 stitches. Join with a slip stitch to form a ring.

Round 1: Chain 1, single crochet twelve times into the center of the ring, join with a slip stitch.

Round 2: Chain 1, (single crochet twice into the next stitch, single crochet once into the next stitch), repeat to the end of the round. Join with a slip stitch.

Round 3: Chain 1, (single crochet twice into the next stitch, single crochet once into both of the following 2 stitches), repeat to the end of the round. Join with a slip stitch. Repeat until you have two bases in each of the three colors.

SIDE

With Sugar, Double Chocolate, or Shell and two double-pointed needles used as straight needles, cast on 6 stitches. Work in garter stitch until the side measures 5 inches or the length required to fit around the edge of the base. Bind off. Cut the yarn and thread it into a yarn needle. Whipstitch the edge of the side to the edge of the base, and join the resulting seam on the side. Stuff with fiberfill.

Repeat until two sides and bases in all three colors are assembled.

TOP (make 6)

With the size G crochet hook and Bleached, chain 6 stitches. Join with a slip stitch to form a ring. Repeat rounds 1 through 3 from the base. Continue as follows:

Round 4: Chain 1, (single crochet twice into the next stitch, single crochet once in each of the following 3 stitches), repeat to the end of the round.

Work the picot edging round from the cake plate in Bleached.

CHERRIES (make 1)

With two double-pointed needles used as straight needles and Rosso, cast on 1 stitch *loosely*, leaving a 3-inch tail.

Row 1: kfb until 5 stitches are on the right needle.
Row 2: Knit.
Row 3: Purl.
Row 4: Knit, do not turn, pass the second, third, fourth, and fifth stitches over the first stitch to create a bobble. Cut the yarn and thread into a yarn needle. Stuff the bobble with the tail from the cast-on. Gather up the edges with stitches and pull tight. Sew one cherry to the center circle of the top of each cupcake.

FINISHING

Place one top over each stuffed cupcake bottom. Sew together using a strand of Bleached and a yarn needle, with the running stitch (see p. 157). The stitching should fall just inside of the picot edge.

sugar bowl

BASE

With the size G crochet hook and Shell, work rounds 1 through 4 from the base and top of the mini-cupcake.

SIDE (make 2)

With two double-pointed needles used as straight needles and Shell, cast on 39 stitches. Work in seed stitch (k1, p1), repeat across every row until the side measures 2 inches.

After completing both sides, whipstitch the pieces together on all four sides to create one piece that is a doubled thickness. Whipstitch the side to the outer edge of the base and sew the side seam.

LID

top • With the size G crochet hook and Bleached, work rounds 1 through 4 from the base and top of the mini-cupcake. Continue as follows:
Round 5: Chain 1, (single crochet twice into the next stitch, single crochet once into each

of the following 4 stitches), repeat to the end of the round. Join with a slip stitch.
Round 6: Chain 1, (single crochet twice into the next stitch, single crochet once into each of the following 5 stitches), repeat to the end of the round. Join with a slip stitch.
Work the picot edging round from the mini-cupcake.

underside of the lid • With the size G crochet hook and Bleached, work rounds 1 through 4 from the base and top of the mini-cupcake. Continue as follows:
Round 5: Chain 1, (single crochet twice into the next stitch, single crochet once into each of the following 4 stitches), repeat to the end of the round. Join with a slip stitch.

Stuff the top of the lid with fiberfill so it is slightly rounded, and place the underside of the lid over the stuffing. Sew together using a length of Bleached and a yarn needle, with the running stitch just inside of the picot edging.

CHERRY

With the size G crochet hook and Rosso, leave a 6-inch end and chain 4 stitches. Join in a ring with a slip stitch. Work in the round as follows:
Round 1: Single crochet six times into the center of the ring, join with a slip stitch.
Round 2: (single crochet twice into the next stitch, single crochet once in the following stitch), repeat to the end of the round, join with a slip stitch.
Round 3: Single crochet once in each of the stitches, join with a slip stitch.
Round 4 (decrease round): single crochet once in every other stitch to the end of the round.

Stuff with fiberfill until the cherry is firm. Cut the yarn, leaving a 6-inch tail and pull through the last stitch. Thread the tail into a yarn needle and gather up both ends of the cherry with a running stitch. Weave ends to the inside and trim. Sew the cherry to the top of the lid.

sugar cubes (make 4)

You will create a piece that is shaped like a lowercase *t* and fold it up like a box to make these small cubes (*illustration below*).

With two double-pointed needles used as straight needles and Bleached, cast on 3 stitches.

Rows 1 and 2: Knit.

Row 3: k3, cast on 3 stitches. (6 stitches.)

Row 4: k6, cast on 3 stitches. (9 stitches.)

Rows 5 and 6: Knit.

Row 7: Bind off 3 stitches, k6. 6 stitches remain.

Row 8: Bind off 3 stitches, k3. 3 stitches remain.

Rows 9–14: Knit.

Bind off. Cut yarn, leaving a long tail. Using the illustration as a guide, fold, sew, and stuff to form a sugar cube.

Store the completed cubes in the cupcake sugar bowl.

SUGAR CUBE

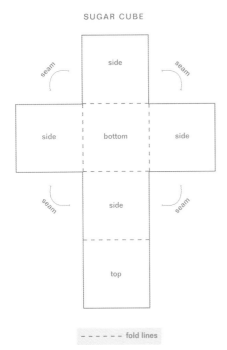

- - - - - - fold lines

teacups (make 2)

TIP • A technique called the jogless jog (see p. 146) is perfect for this type of project. It creates a seamless transition when you are switching colors when working stripes in the round. You don't need to use this technique if you don't mind the visible jog in the stripes; it's up to you.

With four double-pointed needles and Bleached, cast on 30 stitches, distributing 10 stitches on each of three needles. Place a stitch marker and join, making sure the the stitches aren't twisted.

Round 1: Seed stitch (k1, p1) to the end of the round.

Round 2: Seed stitch (p1, k1) to the end of the round.

Switch to Sugar and stockinette stitch, begin stripe pattern as follows:

STRIPE PATTERN

2 rounds Sugar

2 rounds Shell

Knit every round in the stripe pattern until the cup measures 1½ inches from the beginning. Begin the decrease rounds as follows:

DECREASE ROUNDS

Round 1: (k3, k2tog), repeat to the end of the round. 8 stitches per needle remain. 24 stitches total.

Round 2: (k2, k2tog), repeat to the end of the round. 6 stitches per needle remain. 18 stitches total.

Round 3: (k1, k2tog), repeat to the end of the round. 4 stitches per needle remain. 12 stitches total.

Work the rest of the rounds in Bleached.
Rounds 4–7: Knit.

Begin the increase rounds.

Round 8: (k1, kfb), repeat to the end of the round. 6 stitches per needle. 18 stitches total.
Round 9: Knit.
Round 10: (k2, kfb), repeat to the end of the round. 8 stitches per needle. 24 stitches total.
Round 11: Knit.
Round 12: (k3, kfb), repeat to the end of the round. 10 stitches per needle. 30 stitches total.
Round 13: Knit.
Bind off.

With the size D crochet hook and Sugar, complete the picot edging round from the cake plate.

With the size D crochet hook and Bleached, work rounds 1 through 4 of the base and top of

the mini-cupcake. With a length of Bleached and a yarn needle, sew the base to the underside of the teacup with the whipstitch for added support.

With two double-pointed needles used as straight needles and Sugar, cast on 3 stitches. Make I-cord for 2¾ inches. Bind off.

Attach the handle by sewing the cord to the cup for ½ inch along the bottom of the handle. Sew the top of the handle to the cup for ¼ inch. With a long strand of Sugar, tightly wrap the handle as shown in the photograph on page 129. Weave in ends and trim.

teaspoons (make 2)

Make four pieces as follows:

With two double-pointed needles used as straight needles and metallic yarn, cast on 3 stitches. Knit 1 row.
Next row: kfb, k1, kfb. (5 stitches.)
Work in garter stitch until the spoon measures ¾ inches from the beginning.
Next row: ssk, k1, k2tog. 3 stitches remain.
Work in garter stitch until the spoon measures 2 inches from the beginning.

Next row: kfb, k1, kfb. (5 stitches.)
Next row: kfb, k3, kfb. (7 stitches.)
Work in garter stitch until the spoon measures
2¾ inches from the beginning.
Next row: ssk, k3, k2tog. 5 stitches remain.
Knit 1 row.
Next row: ssk, k1, k2tog. 3 stitches remain.
Bind off.

After completing four such pieces, take a pipe
cleaner and make a loop on the end that will
fit inside the basin of the spoon, leaving about
¼ inch of space from the edge. Wrap the end
around to hold the loop in place. Laying the pipe
cleaner on the knitted spoon piece, trim the
other end to fit inside the length of the spoon.
Lay a second piece on top of the pipe cleaner
and whipstitch around the edges of the spoon
with a length of the metallic yarn threaded into a
yarn needle. Repeat with the other two pieces to
make the second spoon.

creamer

With four double-pointed needles and Bleached,
cast on 40 stitches, distributing them onto three
of the needles as follows:
Needles 1 and 2: 15 stitches.
Needle 3: 10 stitches.
Place a stitch marker and join to work in the round.
Work 2 rounds in seed stitch:
Round 1: (k1, p1) to the end of the round.
Round 2: (p1, k1) to the end of the round.

Switch to stockinette stitch and Shell, and begin
the stripe pattern.

STRIPE PATTERN
2 rounds Shell
2 rounds Bleached

> REMINDER • Use the jogless jog technique
> described on page 148 here if you choose.

Work in the stripe pattern until the creamer
measures 2 inches from the beginning.

DECREASE ROUNDS
Round 1: (k3, k2tog), repeat to the end of the
round. 32 stitches remain.
Needles 1 and 2: 12 stitches.
Needle 3: 8 stitches.
Round 2: (k2, k2tog), repeat to the end of the
round. 24 stitches remain.
Needles 1 and 2: 9 stitches.
Needle 3: 6 stitches.
Round 3: (k1, k2tog), repeat to the end of the
round. 16 stitches remain.
Needles 1 and 2: 6 stitches.
Needle 3: 4 stitches.

Switch to using only Bleached.
Rounds 4–7: Knit.

INCREASE ROUNDS
Round 8: (k1, kfb), repeat to the end of the
round. 24 stitches.
Needles 1 and 2: 9 stitches.
Needle 3: 6 stitches.
Round 9: Knit.
Round 10: (k2, kfb), repeat to the end of the
round. 32 stitches.
Needles 1 and 2: 12 stitches.
Needle 3: 6 stitches.
Round 11: Knit.
Round 12: (k3, kfb), repeat to the end of the
round. 40 stitches.
Needles 1 and 2: 15 stitches.
Needle 3: 10 stitches.
Round 13: Knit.
Bind off.

With the size D crochet hook and Shell, work the
picot edging round from the cake plate.

BASE
With the size D crochet hook and Bleached,
work rounds 1 through 4 from the base and top
of the mini-cupcake. Continue as follows:
Round 5: Chain 1 stitch (single crochet twice into

On the opposite side of the base from the handle, pinch together a ½ inch tuck, and secure with a few whipstitches of Bleached, to form the spout. Pinch the top edge together to define the spout further.

TEA BAGS (make 2)

Due to choking hazards (small stickers and sequins), make these only for children over three years old.

With two double-pointed needles used as straight needles and Grace, cast on 10 stitches. Work in stockinette stitch until the bag measures 2 inches. Bind off. Fold the bag in half so the cast-on edge meets the bound-off edge. Fill the bag partially full with sequins and whipstitch the edges together with a length of Grace threaded into a yarn needle.

With the size D crochet hook, chain stitch for 4 inches. Attach the chain to the center of the seamed edge. Put two flower stickers back to back on the end of the chain to form a tag.

teapot

BASE

With two double-pointed needles used as straight needles and Bleached, cast on 5 stitches.

Row 1: kfb, k3, kfb. (7 stitches.)
Row 2 and all following even rows: Purl.
Row 3: kfb, k5, kfb. (9 stitches.)
Row 5: kfb, k7, kfb. (11 stitches.)
Row 7: kfb, k9, kfb. (13 stitches.)
Row 9: kfb, k11, kfb. (15 stitches.)
Row 11: Knit.
Row 13: Knit.
Row 15: ssk, k11, k2tog. 13 stitches remain.
Row 17: ssk, k9, k2tog. 11 stitches remain.
Row 19: ssk, k7, k2tog. 9 stitches remain.
Row 21: ssk, k5, k2tog. 7 stitches remain.
Row 23: ssk, k3, k2tog. 5 stitches remain.
Do not bind off.

the next stitch, single crochet once into each of the following 4 stitches), repeat to the end of the round. Join the round with a slip stitch.

Round 6: Chain 1 stitch (single crochet twice into the next stitch, single crochet once into each of the following 5 stitches), repeat to the end of the round. Join the round with a slip stitch.

Sew the base to the underside of the bottom of the creamer. Using a length of Bleached threaded into a yarn needle and a running stitch, sew just inside the picot edge.

HANDLE

With two double-pointed needles used as straight needles and Shell, cast on 3 stitches. Make I-cord for 3½ inches. Bind off.

Attach the handle by sewing the cord to the cup for ½ inch along the bottom of the handle. Sew the top of the handle to the cup for ¼ inch. With a long strand of Sugar, tightly wrap the handle as for the teacups.

BODY

Leave these 5 stitches on the needle, turn the work clockwise, and with the same needle pick up and knit 6 stitches along the edge. (11 stitches.) With three other double-pointed needles, continue picking up and knitting stitches around the edges of the base until there are 11 stitches on each of the needles. (44 stitches.) Place a marker and knit 1 round. On the next round, increase 4 stitches on each of the four needles as follows:

Next round: On each needle: k1, kfb, k3, kfb, k3, kfb, k3, kfb, k1. 14 stitches per needle. 56 stitches total.

Begin the stripe pattern.

STRIPE PATTERN

2 rounds Shell
2 rounds Sugar
2 rounds Bleached

Next round: Starting the stripe pattern with Shell, on each needle work as follows:
(k1, kfb, knit to the last 2 stitches, kfb, k1). 16 stitches remain on each needle. 64 stitches total. Work in the stripe pattern for 4 inches from the pickup round.

Change to Bleached and begin the decrease rounds as follows:

Round 1: (k6, k2tog), repeat to the end of the round. 14 stitches per needle remain. 56 stitches total.

Round 2: (k5, k2tog), repeat to the end of the round. 12 stitches per needle remain. 48 stitches total.

Round 3: Knit.

Round 4: (k4, k2tog), repeat to the end of the round. 10 stitches per needle remain. 40 stitches total.

Round 5: Knit.

Round 6: (k3, k2tog), repeat to the end of the round. 8 stitches per needle remain. 32 stitches total.

Round 7: (k2, k2tog), repeat to the end of the round. 6 stitches per needle remain. 24 stitches total.

Round 8: (k1, k2tog), repeat to the end of the round. 4 stitches per needle remain. 16 stitches total.

Round 9: k2tog, repeat to the end of the round. 2 stitches per needle remain. 8 stitches total.

Fill the teapot with poly-pellets until it is half full. Fill the rest with fiberfill until the teapot is firm. Cut the yarn and thread into a yarn needle. Pull tail through the remaining live stitches and gather up tight. Secure and weave in end.

LID

With the size D crochet hook and Bleached, work rounds 1 through 4 from the base and top of the mini-cupcake. Continue as follows:

Round 5: Chain 1 stitch (single crochet twice into the next stitch, single crochet once into each of the following 4 stitches), repeat to the end of the round. Slip stitch to join the round. Work the picot edging round from the cake plate.

CHERRY

Work as for the sugar bowl cherry and sew it to the center circle of the lid.

Sew the lid to the top of the teapot using a running stitch, just inside of the picot edging.

HANDLE (make 2)

With two double-pointed needles and Bleached, cast on 6 stitches. Make I-cord for 5 inches. Fold a pipe cleaner in half and push the folded end inside of the I-cord tube. Trim the ends to fit inside the cord. Bind off.

Repeat for the second handle.

Sew the handles onto the side of the teapot side by side, stitching down ½ inch of the I-cord at the bottom of the handle to the pot. Turn the handles under at the top and sew down for ¼ inch. With a long length of Sugar threaded into a yarn needle, tightly wrap the two handles together in a figure eight pattern, going over, under, and in between the handles with the yarn. Weave the end through the wrapping for about an inch to secure, then trim.

SPOUT

With two double-pointed needles used as straight needles and Sugar, cast on 5 stitches.

Row 1: kfb, k3, kfb. (7 stitches.)

Row 2 and all following even rows: Purl.

Row 3: kfb, k5, kfb. (9 stitches.)

Row 5: kfb, k7, kfb. (11 stitches.)

Row 7: kfb, k9, kfb. (13 stitches.)

Row 9: kfb, k11, kfb. (15 stitches.)

Transfer the stitches onto three double-pointed needles, 5 stitches per needle. The fourth needle will now be your working needle. Place a marker and join, making sure the stitches aren't twisted. Knit every round until the spout measures 1½ inches from the beginning.

Work 2 rounds in seed stitch:

Round 1: (k1, p1), repeat to the end of the round.

Round 2: (p1, k1), repeat to the end of the round. Bind off.

Sew the nonribbed end of the spout to the teapot, increases pointing down, with Sugar and a yarn needle. Whipstitch in place, weave in the ends, and trim.

dotted chickens

Chickens—why the obsession? I couldn't possibly explain it. I am not fond of *real* chickens, just those with polka dots! I made one of these hens and loved it so much, I had to make a second one immediately. They look good together, no? Best friends forever!

yarn

- Rowan Handknit Cotton (100% cotton; 93 yards/50 grams), 1 skein each of Bleached #263, Sugar #303, Celery #309, Slick #313, Mango Fool #319, Seafarer #318, and Buttercup #320

tools

- U.S. size 3 set of five double-pointed needles or size needed to obtain gauge
- One skein of black embroidery floss
- Small bag of polyester fiberfill
- Small bag of poly-pellets
- Stitch marker
- Scissors
- Yarn needle
- Ruler or tape measure

gauge

- 6 stitches per inch

BASE

With two double-pointed needles used as straight needles and Bleached, cast on 5 stitches.

Row 1: kfb, k3, kfb. (7 stitches.)
Row 2 and all following even rows: Purl.
Row 3: kfb, k5, kfb. (9 stitches.)
Row 5: kfb, k7, kfb. (11 stitches.)
Row 7: kfb, k9, kfb. (13 stitches.)
Row 9: kfb, k11, kfb. (15 stitches.)
Row 11: Knit.
Row 13: Knit.
Row 15: ssk, k11, k2tog. 13 stitches remain.
Row 17: ssk, k9, k2tog. 11 stitches remain.
Row 19: ssk, k7, k2tog. 9 stitches remain.
Row 21: ssk, k5, k2tog. 7 stitches remain.
Row 23: ssk, k3, k2tog. 5 stitches remain.
Do not bind off.

BODY

Leaving these 5 stitches on the needle and continuing with the same needle, turn the work clockwise and pick up and knit 6 stitches along the edge. (11 stitches.) With the other three double-pointed needles, continue picking up and knitting stitches until you have 11 stitches on each of the needles. (44 stitches.)
Place a marker and knit 1 round.
On the next round, increase 4 stitches on each of the 4 needles as follows:

Increase round: k1, kfb, k3, kfb, k3, kfb, k3, kfb, k1. 14 stitches per needle. 56 stitches total.

Knit every round until body measures 2½ inches from the pickup round. Start the decrease sequence for the neck.

DECREASE ROUNDS

Round 1: On each needle, (k5, k2tog) 2 times. 12 stitches per needle remain. 48 stitches total.
Round 2: Knit.
Round 3: On each needle, (k4, k2tog) 2 times. 10 stitches per needle remain. 40 stitches total.
Round 4: Knit.
Round 5: On each needle, (k3, k2tog) 2 times. 8 stitches per needle remain. 32 stitches total.
Round 6: On each needle, (k2, k2tog) 2 times. 6 stitches per needle remain. 24 stitches total.
Round 7: On each needle, (k1, k2tog) 2 times. 4 stitches per needle remain. 16 stitches total.
Pour poly-pellets into the body until it is about half full. Then stuff with the fiberfill until the body is firm.
Round 8: On needle 1, k2, k2tog; on needles 2 and 3, knit to the end of the round. 15 stitches total remain.

Distribute the 15 remaining stitches evenly to three double-pointed needles, 5 stitches per needle.

NECK AND HEAD

Rounds 1–3: Knit.

Round 4: On each needle, k3, k2tog. 4 stitches per needle remain. 12 stitches total.

Rounds 5–7: Knit.

Round 8: On each needle, k1 (m1, k1) 3 times. 7 stitches per needle. 21 stitches total.

Rounds 9–13: Knit.

Round 14: On each needle, ssk, k3, k2tog. 5 stitches per needle remain. 15 stitches total.

Rounds 15 and 16: Knit.

Round 17: On each needle, ssk, k1, k2tog. 3 stitches per needle remain. 9 stitches total. Stuff the neck and head with the fiberfill until firm. Cut the yarn and thread the tail into a yarn needle. Pull through the remaining live stitches and pull tight to gather. Secure and weave the end to the inside.

TAIL

With two double-pointed needles used as straight needles and Bleached, cast on 8 stitches.

Row 1: Knit.

Row 2: Knit to the last stitch, kfb. (9 stitches.)

Row 3: kfb, knit to the end of the row. (10 stitches.)

Row 4: Knit to the last stitch, kfb. (11 stitches.)

Row 5: kfb, knit to the end of the row. (12 stitches.)

Row 6: Knit to the last stitch, kfb. (13 stitches.)

Row 7: Bind off 5 stitches, knit to the end of the row. 8 stitches remain.

Row 8: Knit.

Repeat rows 1 through 8 three more times until four points have been completed. Bind off all stitches. Cut the yarn and thread the tail into a yarn needle. Lap the angled end of the tail over the straight end to form a ring and stitch in place using whipstitch. Sew the tail onto the body. Weave in all ends and trim.

BOBBLES (make 4)

With two double-pointed needles used as straight needles and either Seafarer or Slick, cast on 1 stitch *loosely*, leaving a 1-inch tail.

Row 1: kfb until 3 stitches are on the right needle.

Row 2: Knit.

Row 3: Purl.

Row 4: Knit, do not turn, pass the second and third stitches over the first stitch to form a bobble. Cut the yarn and thread the tail into a yarn needle. Stuff the bobble with the 1-inch tail and gather up with stitches. Pull tight and sew one bobble on each of the four points of the tail. Pull the points so that they curl outward.

HEAD RUFFLE

With two double-pointed needles used as straight needles and Sugar or Seafarer, cast on 4 stitches.

Row 1: Knit.

Row 2: Bind off 2 stitches, k2. 2 stitches remain.

Row 3: k2, cast on 2 stitches. 4 stitches remain.

Row 4: Bind off 2 stitches, k2. 2 stitches remain.

Row 5: k2, cast on 2 stitches. (4 stitches.)

Row 6: Bind off all stitches.

Cut yarn and pull through the last stitch. Thread tail into yarn needle and sew the ruffle to the top of the head in whichever direction you want the hen to be looking, using a whipstitch.

BEAKS (make 2)

With two double-pointed needles used as straight needles and Slick or Seafarer, cast on 1 stitch *loosely*.

Row 1: kfb. (2 stitches.)

Row 2: Knit, do not turn, pass the second stitch over the first stitch.

Cut yarn and gather piece into a tiny bobble.

Sew bobbles onto the head in line with the head ruffle.

EYES

With black embroidery floss threaded into a yarn needle, make two V-shaped eyes by following

the shape of 1 knit stitch on either side of the beak.

DOTS

For the chicken with the Slick beak, head ruffle, and tail bobbles make dots as follows:

Large Dots	Small Dots
2 Sugar	2 Buttercup
2 Seafarer	3 Celery
3 Mango Fool	1 Sugar

For the hen with the Seafarer beak, head ruffle, and tail bobbles make the same small dots, and for the large dots, use Slick instead of Seafarer.

large dot • With two double-pointed needles used as straight needles and color required, cast on 1 stitch.

Row 1: kfb until you have 3 stitches on the right needle.
Row 2: kfb, k1, kfb. (5 stitches.)
Row 3: Purl.
Row 4: Knit.

Row 5: Purl.
Row 6: ssk, k1, k2tog. 3 stitches remain. Do not turn, pass the second and third stitches over the 1st stitch.

Cut the yarn, leaving a 6-inch tail, and pull through the remaining stitch.

small dot • With two double-pointed needles used as straight needles and color required, cast on 1 stitch.

Row 1: kfb until you have 3 stitches on the right needle.
Row 2: Purl.
Row 3: Knit.
Row 4: Purl.
Row 5: Knit, do not turn, pass the second and third stitches over the first stitch.

Cut the yarn, leaving a 6-inch tail, and pull through the remaining stitch. Thread the dot tails into a yarn needle and sew the dots flat all over the body and tail with the whipstitch. Invisibly weave in ends and trim.

three pigs and a wolf

I love the idea of finger puppets, but without a story, sometimes they aren't as fun to play with. That's why I knitted this adaptation of a classic fairytale—you know the one: I'll huff and I'll puff, and something about hair on my chinny-chin-chin. I just had to include three little huts, a chimney, and a big black cooking pot to boot! Use them to have a great, imaginative time with your favorite child.

yarn

- Rowan Handknit Cotton (100% cotton; 93 yards/50 grams), 2 skeins in Rosso #215; 1 skein each in Chime #204, Bleached #263, Double Chocolate #315, Shell #310, and Linen #205

tools

- U.S. size 3 set of four double-pointed needles or size needed to obtain gauge
- U.S. size 3 24-inch circular needle, or size needed to obtain gauge
- U.S. size 3 16-inch circular needle, or size needed to obtain gauge
- U.S. size E crochet hook
- One skein of black embroidery floss
- Two stitch holders
- Stitch marker
- Scissors
- Yarn needle
- Ruler or tape measure

gauge

- 6 stitches per inch

pigs (make 3)

BODY AND HEAD

With three double-pointed needles and Shell, cast on 15 stitches, 5 stitches per needle. Place marker and join, making sure that the stitches aren't twisted. Work in stockinette stitch until piece measures 2 inches. Begin the decrease rounds for the head.

DECREASE ROUNDS

Round 1: On each needle, k3, k2tog. 4 stitches per needle remain. 12 stitches total.
Round 2: Knit.
Round 3: On each needle, k2, k2tog. 3 stitches per needle remain. 9 stitches total.
Round 4: Knit.
Round 5: On each needle, k1, k2tog. 2 stitches per needle remain. 6 stitches total.

Cut yarn and thread the tail into a yarn needle. Pull the tail through the remaining live stitches, gather tight, and secure. Weave end to the inside and trim. The cast-on edge is left open so the puppet can be placed on the finger.

SNOUT

Using two double-pointed needles as straight needles and Shell, cast on 1 stitch *loosely*. Knit into the front, back, and front again until there are 3 stitches on the right needle.
Row 1: Knit.
Row 2: Purl.
Row 3: Knit, do not turn, pass the second and third stitches over the first stitch.

Cut the yarn, leaving a 6-inch tail, and pull through the remaining stitch. Thread tail into a yarn needle. Form snout into a round shape and whipstitch this piece over the gathered end of the body. Weave in the end on the inside and trim.

EARS (make 2)

Using two double-pointed needles as straight needles and Shell, cast on 3 stitches, leaving a 4-inch tail.
Row 1: Knit.

Row 2: ssk, k1, pass second stitch over the first stitch.

Cut the yarn and pull through the last stitch. Thread tail from the cast-on edge into a yarn needle. Sew the ears to the head of the pig with the whipstitch.

LEGS (make 4)

Using two double-pointed needles as straight needles and Shell, cast on 1 stitch *loosely*, leaving a 1-inch tail. Knit into the front, back, and front again so that there are 3 stitches on the right needle.

Row 1: Knit.
Row 2: Purl.
Row 3: Knit, do not turn, pass the second and third stitches over the first stitch. Cut the yarn and pull through the remaining stitch to create a bobble. Thread tail into a yarn needle, stuff the bobble with the tail from the cast-on, and gather the edges to form a ball.

Sew the four bobbles to the underside of the pig to create stubby legs.

TAIL

Using two double-pointed needles as straight needles and Shell, cast on 7 stitches. Bind off tightly. Sew one end to the back of the pig and give it a twist with your fingers.

EYES

With black embroidery floss take 2 stitches for eyes.

wolf

BODY AND HEAD

With Chime, work as for the pig up to the decrease rounds. Change to Bleached and complete the head as for the pig.

EARS

With Chime, work the ears as for the pig.

TAIL

Using two double-pointed needles as straight needles and Chime, cast on 3 stitches.
Row 1: Knit.
Row 2: Purl.
Rows 3–6: Repeat rows 1 and 2 two more times.
Row 7: k1, k2tog, pass the second stitch over the first stitch. With the yarn end threaded into a yarn needle, sew the tail onto the back of the wolf.

LEGS (make 4)

Using two double-pointed needles and Chime, cast on 3 stitches. Make I-cord for ½ inch. Bind off. Repeat three more times and sew the legs onto the underside of the wolf with the yarn tail threaded into a yarn needle.

FEET (make 4)

Using two double-pointed needles as straight needles and Bleached, cast on 6 stitches.
Rows 1–4: (k1, sl1 with yarn in back as if to purl), repeat across the row.
Cut the yarn and thread the tail into a yarn needle. Pull the yarn needle through the live stitches and pull up tight. Repeat three times and sew the feet to the bottom of the legs.

EYES AND NOSE

Use the photograph as a guide and with black embroidery floss and a yarn needle, take 2 little stitches for eyes and several stitches for the nose.

huts

STRAW HUT

back • With the 24-inch circular needle and Linen, cast on 30 stitches. Working back and forth on the needles, begin basket weave pattern.

BASKET WEAVE PATTERN

Rows 1–6: (k 5, p 5) to the end of the row.

Rows 7–12: (p 5, k 5) to the end of the row. Continue repeating rows 1 through 12 until back measures 3½ inches. Place stitches on a holder and set aside.

front • With the 24-inch circular needle and Linen, cast on 10 stitches. Work the basket weave pattern as for the back for 2 inches. Cut the yarn, place the stitches on a holder, and set aside. Repeat, working for 2 inches, but do not cut the yarn.

Next row: Work across the 10 stitches on the needle, cast on 10 stitches using the backward-loop method, work the 10 stitches from the holder. (30 stitches).

Continue in the basket weave pattern until piece measures 3½ inches. Do not cut the yarn.

Sew the front and back together along the sides.

roof • With side seams sewn, place the 60 live stitches on three double-pointed needles, distributing them equally, 20 stitches per needle. Place a marker where your yarn is attached. Join, making sure the stitches aren't twisted.

Round 1: Knit.
Rounds 2 and 3: Purl.
Round 4: (k2, k2tog), repeat to the end of the round. 16 stitches per needle remain. 48 stitches total.
Rounds 5–8: Knit.
Round 9: (k2, k2tog), repeat to the end of the round. 12 stitches per needle remain. 36 stitches total.
Rounds 10–12: Knit.
Round 13: (k1, k2tog), repeat to the end of the round. 8 stitches per needle remain. 24 stitches total.
Rounds 14–16: Knit.
Round 17: k2tog, repeat to the end of the round. 4 stitches per needle remain. 12 stitches total.
Round 18: k2tog, repeat to the end of the round. 2 stitches per needle remain. 6 stitches total.
Cut the yarn, thread into a yarn needle, and pull through the remaining live stitches. Pull up tight, and secure, weave in end on the inside, and trim.

With the crochet hook and Linen, single crochet around the door opening.

straw tassel • Make a 2-inch tassel with 20 wraps (see p. 153) and sew to the top of the hut so it stands straight up.

HUT OF STICKS
back • With the 24-inch circular needle and Double Chocolate, cast on 20 stitches.
Row 1: Knit.
Row 2: Purl.
Row 3: Knit.
Row 4: Knit (to create turning row).
Rows 5–7: Repeat rows 1 through 3.
Row 8: Knit.
Row 9: Purl.
Rows 10 and 11: Repeat rows 8 and 9.
Row 12: Purl.
Row 13: Knit.
Repeat rows 8 through 13 until piece measures 3½ inches from the beginning, ending with a wrong side row. Do not bind off.

Place 5 of the stitches from the circular needle on one double-pointed needle and make I-cord for 3 inches. Bind off. Reattach the yarn and repeat the process with the next 5 stitches on the circular needle. Repeat until you have six I-cords at the top of the back.

Turn the hem under at the turning row and whipstitch into place, using a yarn needle and a length of Double Chocolate.

front • With the 24-inch circular needle and Double Chocolate, cast on 10 stitches. Work as for back until the front measures 2 inches from the beginning, ending with a wrong side row. Cut the yarn and place stitches on a holder. Set aside.

Repeat, but do not cut the yarn.

Next row: Keeping in pattern, work across the 10 stitches on the needle, cast on 10 stitches

using the backward-loop method, work across the 10 stitches from the holder. 30 stitches total. Continue in pattern and work until front measures 3½ inches from the beginning, ending with a wrong side row. Complete as for back. Turn the hem under at the turning row and whipstitch into place. Sew side seams, using the mattress stitch. Gather up the I-cords and sew them together about an inch from the top to form the roof.

With the crochet hook, single crochet around the front opening.

BRICK HUT

back • With the 24-inch circular needle, and Rosso, cast on 40 stitches. Begin brick pattern.

BRICK PATTERN

Row 1: (k4, p4) to the end of the row.
Row 2: Repeat row 1.
Row 3: (p4, k4) to the end of the row.
Row 4: Repeat row 3.

Repeat rows 1 through 4 until back measures 5 inches from the beginning. Cut yarn and place stitches on a holder.

front • With the 24-inch circular needle and Rosso, cast on 12 stitches. Repeat rows 1 through 4 from the back until the front measures 3 inches, ending with a wrong side row. Place the stitches on a holder and set aside.
Repeat for the other side of the front, but do not cut the yarn. Keeping in the brick pattern, work across the 12 stitches on the needles, cast on 20 stitches using the backward-loop method, then work across the 12 stitches from the holder. 44 stitches total.
Continue in the brick pattern until the front measures 5 inches.

With a length of yarn and a yarn needle, sew the side seams with the mattress stitch. Turn up the bottom edge ½ inch to the outside and sew into place using the whipstitch. This gives the house a bit more stability.

Transfer all of the live stitches from the front and back to the 16-inch circular needle. 84 stitches total. Place a marker and join, making sure that the stitches aren't twisted.

Round 1: Knit.

Round 2: (k4, k2tog), repeat to the end of the round. 70 stitches remain.

Rounds 3–5: Knit.

Round 6: (k3, k2tog), repeat to the end of the round. 56 stitches remain.

Rounds 7 and 8: Transfer stitches to three double-pointed needles as follows:

Needle 1: 20 stitches.

Needle 2: 20 stitches.

Needle 3: 16 stitches.

Round 9: (k2, k2tog), repeat to the end of the round. 42 stitches remain.

Rounds 10–19: Knit.

Round 20: Purl.

Bind off all stitches.

reinforcement • With the 24-inch circular needle and Rosso, cast on 15 stitches. Work in garter stitch until piece measures 11 inches. Bind off. Sew this piece to the inside of the hut with a whipstitch on all sides to make it sturdier.

black pot

With three double-pointed needles and Black, cast on 50 stitches as follows:

Needle 1: 20 stitches.

Needle 2: 20 stitches.

Needle 3: 10 stitches.

Place a marker and join, making sure the stitches aren't twisted. Purl 1 round. Continue knitting in stockinette stitch until pot measures 1½ inches from the beginning.

Round 1: (k3, k2tog), repeat to the end of the round. 40 stitches remain.

Round 2: (k2, k2tog), repeat to the end of the round. 30 stitches remain.

Round 3: (k1, k2tog), repeat to the end of the round. 20 stitches remain.

Round 4: k2tog, repeat to the end of the round. 10 stitches remain.

Cut the yarn. Thread the tail into a yarn needle and pull through the remaining live stitches. Pull up tight, secure, and weave in the end. Trim.

LEGS (make 3)

Using two double-pointed needles as straight needles and Black, cast on 1 stitch *loosely,* leaving a 2-inch tail. Knit into the front and back of this stitch until there are 5 stitches on the right needle.

Row 1: Knit.

Row 2: Purl.

Row 3: Knit, do not turn, pass the second, third, fourth, and fifth stitches over the first stitch. Cut the yarn and thread into a yarn needle. Stuff the bobble with the tail from the cast-on stitch and gather up the edges with the yarn needle to form a ball.

Repeat two more times and sew bobble legs to the bottom of the pot.

HANDLES (make 2)

With two double-pointed needles and Black, cast on 2 stitches. Make I-cord for 2 inches. Bind off. With a length of yarn and a yarn needle, sew both ends to the top of the pot, using the photograph on page 139 as a guide, to form a handle. Repeat and attach the other handle opposite the first.

a few more stitches

The second stitch to learn in knitting is the purl stitch. The purl stitch is really just a knit stitch worked from the back. After you have the knit stitch down, you can create different stitch patterns and textures in your knitting by combining it with the purl stitch. As with the knit stitch, you'll be taking the stitches from the left needle and working them onto the right needle.

1. Hold the stitches on the left needle with the working yarn in front. Hold the yarn over your left index finger. The tension on the yarn is created by squeezing the yarn between the index and middle finger of your left hand.

2. Insert the right needle from right to left through the front of the first stitch. The points of the needles make an X.

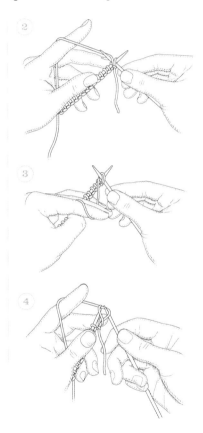

3. With your left index finger, bring the yarn up and over and down behind the right needle. When you bring the yarn down, squeeze it between the index and middle finger of your left hand to keep the yarn taut.

4. Tip the point of the right needle upward and bring the loop back through the stitch and onto the right needle.

5. Slip the completed stitch off the left needle. The new purl stitch is now on the right needle.

Using different stitches creates different looks and textures in your knitting. Once you have the knit and purl stitches mastered, the sky's the limit. The following stitch patterns are the most commonly used throughout the book. For each of them I have provided instructions for knitting back and forth, as well as in the round.

stockinette stitch

(worked over any number of stitches)

BACK AND FORTH

Row 1 (right side): Knit.
Row 2: Purl.
Repeat rows 1 and 2.

IN THE ROUND

Knit every round (knit side is the right side).

garter stitch

(worked over any number of stitches)

BACK AND FORTH

Knit every row.

IN THE ROUND

Round 1: Knit.
Round 2: Purl.
Repeat rounds 1 and 2.

seed stitch

(worked over an even number of stitches)

BACK AND FORTH

Row 1: Knit 1 stitch, purl 1 stitch. Repeat to end of row.
Row 2: Purl 1 stitch, knit 1 stitch. Repeat to end of row.
Repeat rows 1 and 2.

IN THE ROUND

Round 1: Knit 1 stitch, purl 1 stitch. Repeat to end of round.
Round 2: Purl 1 stitch, knit 1 stitch. Repeat to end of round.
Repeat rounds 1 and 2.

basket weave

(worked over any multiple of 4 stitches)

BACK AND FORTH

Row 1: Knit 4 stitches, purl 4 stitches. Repeat to end of row.
Row 2: Knit 4 stitches, purl 4 stitches. Repeat to end of row.
Rows 3 and 4: Repeat rows 1 and 2.
Row 5: Purl 4 stitches, knit 4 stitches. Repeat to end of row.
Row 6: Purl 4 stitches, knit 4 stitches. Repeat to end of row.
Rows 7 and 8: Repeat rows 5 and 6.
Repeat rows 1–8.

IN THE ROUND

Round 1: Knit 4 stitches, purl 4 stitches. Repeat to end of round.
Rounds 2–4: Repeat round 1.
Round 5: Purl 4 stitches, knit 4 stitches. Repeat to end of round.
Rounds 6–8: Repeat to round 5. Repeat rounds 1–8.

special techniques

THE BACKWARD-LOOP METHOD

This type of cast-on is used for casting on in the middle of a row, for casting on at the end of a row, and for making a picot edging. It is simple and easy for children and anyone just learning to knit.

1. Make a slip knot with a short tail about 8 inches long, as you'll only use yarn attached to the ball for casting on with this method. Put the slip knot on the needle and tighten it. Hold the needle in your right hand.

2. Place the working yarn across your left palm (your palm is facing you) and gently put your fingers over the yarn. Wrap the yarn around the outside of your thumb.

3. Imagining your left thumb is your left needle, put the point of the right needle under and through the loop of yarn formed around your thumb.

4. Gently pull your thumb out of the loop and tighten the new stitch on your needle. Wrap the yarn around your thumb.

* Repeat steps 3 and 4 until the desired number of stitches are on your needle.

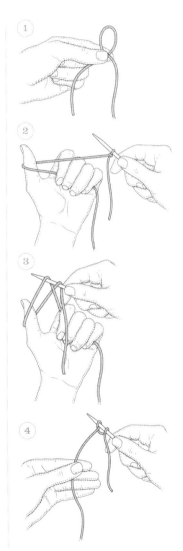

I-cord is a tried and true embellishment that has endless uses. For this collection it is used for buttons and loops, arms and legs, teapot handles, and much more. The versatility of this knitted cord makes it a must for every knitter to learn. Here are the steps for making I-cord:

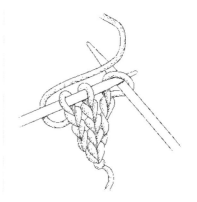

1. Using a double-pointed needle, cast on 2, 3, or 4 stitches, depending on how thick you want your cord. Knit these stitches using another double-pointed needle and *do not turn the work.*

2. Slide the stitches to the other end of the double-pointed needle. The yarn will now be on the opposite side of the work.

3. Bring the yarn very firmly around the back of the work and knit the stitches firmly to create a tube. Do not turn.

Repeat rows 2 and 3 until the cord reaches the desired length. Bind off. Cut the yarn and pull it through the last stitch.

TIP • When knitting I-cord, gently pull down on the cord as it forms. This helps the stitches to fall in place to better form the cord.

PICK UP AND KNIT

To pick up and knit stitches is a basic skill that every knitter needs to master. It is used in the toys and the felted bag, and is an easy way to continue knitting onto another piece of knitted fabric. I also use this technique to pick up the sleeves from the body of a couple of sweaters in this collection.

Pick up and knit means that you will be picking up stitches along an edge or another place on the fabric as if you are going to knit them. This means you will insert the needle into your knitted fabric and wrap the yarn as if you were knitting. Put these new stitches on your right needle. You can use this technique for collars, edgings, and sleeves. Be careful not to create holes as you work by making sure you insert the needle into the correct point on the knitted piece. The pattern will tell you how many stitches to pick up.

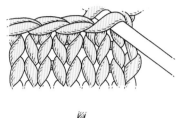

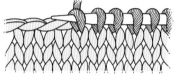

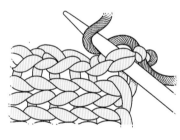

Pick up and knit from a bound-off edge.

1. With the yarn held to the back of your piece and the right side of your work facing you, take one needle in your right hand and insert the needle from front to back (right through the fabric), into each stitch just beneath the cast-on edge, or bind-off edge, or one stitch in on a side edge.

2. Wrap the yarn as if to knit and pull the loop through the fabric, leaving the new stitch on the right needle.

Pick up and knit from a side edge.

JOGLESS JOG

This ingenious technique is a Meg Swansen original, and it is used to disguise the jog between colors when working stripes in the round. You don't have to do this technique if you don't mind the look of steps at the beginning of the round, but it looks much smoother if you do.

1. After you change to a new color when knitting in the round, complete one round in the new color. Note that at the end of the round the last stitch is one round higher than the first stitch of the round.

2. On the first stitch of the next round, lift the stitch below the first stitch, in the previous color, onto the left needle with the tip of the right needle.

3. Then simply knit those two stitches together. The previous color will cover the new color to create an invisible jog in the colors.

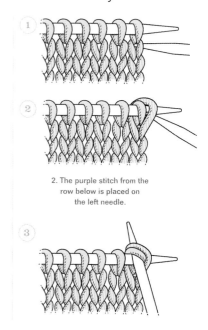

2. The purple stitch from the row below is placed on the left needle.

DECREASING

Decreasing is used when you want to make your piece narrower at a certain point, like at the top of a hat. You do this by making fewer stitches as you go..

KNIT 2 STITCHES TOGETHER

This makes a right-slanting decrease.

1. With the right needle, and the yarn in back, put the point through the first 2 stitches on the left needle at the same time as if to knit.

2. Knit these 2 stitches together to make 1 stitch on the right needle.

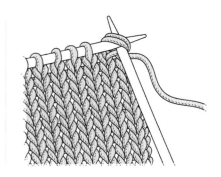

PURL 2 STITCHES TOGETHER

This makes a right-slanting decrease.

1. With the right needle, and the yarn in front, put the point through the first 2 stitches on the left needle at the same time as if to purl.

2. Purl these 2 stitches together to make 1 stitch on the right needle.

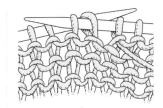

SLIP STITCH, SLIP STITCH, KNIT 2 STITCHES TOGETHER THROUGH THE BACK LOOPS, OR SSK (SLIP, SLIP, KNIT)

This makes a left-slanting decrease.

1. With the right needle and the yarn in back of the work, slip the first 2 stitches onto the right needle as if to knit.

2. With the left needle, put the point through the front of the 2 slipped stitches on the right needle.

3. Knit the 2 slipped stitches together by wrapping the yarn around the right needle and pulling a loop through onto the right needle, making 1 stitch on the right needle.

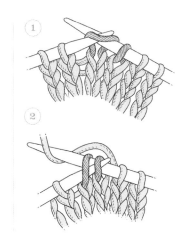

INCREASING

Increases are used when you want to make your knitted piece wider. You do this by adding stitches as you go.

KNIT IN THE FRONT AND BACK OF THE SAME STITCH

1. Knit the first stich and leave it on the left needle.

2. Insert the tip of the right needle into the back of the same stitch and knit again.

3. Slip the stitch off the left needle. Two stitches have been made from 1 stitch and are now on the right needle.

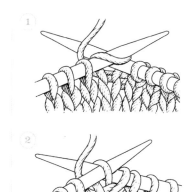

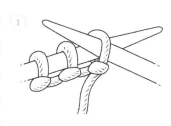

PURL IN THE FRONT AND BACK OF THE SAME STITCH

1. Purl the first stitch and leave it on the left needlle.

2. Insert the tip of the right needle through the back of the same stitch from left to right and bring the point to the front. Purl again.

3. Slip the stitch off the left needle. Two stitches have been made from 1 stitch and are now on the right needle.

FINISHING TECHNIQUES

3-NEEDLE BIND-OFF

This is a slick technique used to seam and bind off at the same time. I have used the 3-needle bind-off in this collection for shoulder seams on sweaters. It works great, and you don't have to seam after you are finished knitting. You'll discover how easy it is.

> TIP • Have a third needle handy before you begin, as the title points out.

1. Turn the project inside out.

2. Divide the stitches to be joined evenly onto two needles and hold both of these needles parallel in your left hand. For this bind-off, you have to have the same number of stitches on each needle. The points of both needles are right next to each other and pointing to the right.

3. With the third needle, knit through the first stitch on both parallel needles and knit them together, making 1 stitch on the right needle. Repeat this so there are 2 stitches on the right needle. Your tension should match the tension of the rest of the knitting; do not work too tightly unless the rest of the piece is worked tightly.

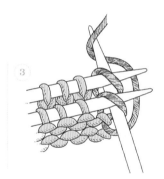

4. On the right needle, pass the right stitch over the left stitch and off the needle.

5. Knit through the next stitches on both left needles, making 1 more stitch on the right needle, and repeat step 4.

Repeat steps 4 and 5 until 1 stitch remains on the right needle. Cut the yarn, leaving a tail. Pull the tail through the last stitch, and pull it tight. Turn your project right side out and marvel at the beautiful seam you've just made!

MATTRESS STITCH

This is a great technique for making an invisible seam. I used it on the sides of sweaters as well as on Baby's Texture Blanket.

1. Lay the pieces flat with the right sides facing up. Pin the pieces together with safety pins if necessary. Thread a tail end or new piece of yarn through a yarn needle, and begin sewing at the bottom of the seam.

2. Working upward, find the bars, or horizontal strands, between the first stitch and second stitch up the sides of the pieces. You can do this by gently pulling apart the two stitches.

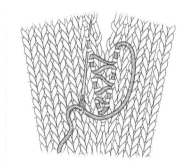

3. Put the needle under the first two bars on one side and draw the yarn through. Then place it under the two bars directly opposite on the other piece and draw the yarn through. Repeat back and forth this way, working up the seam two bars at a time on each side. As you go, be sure to insert the needle into the last "hole" you came out of on each side.

• Complete by weaving in the end along the seam on the inside of the piece.

BLOCKING

I have to make a confession: for the projects in this book, I didn't do any blocking. Every sample in the book is completely unblocked, as I love handknit items to look, well, handknit. I know for lace and certain other projects, you really do have to block, so with that being said, let me tell you how I go about it. Note that blocking will only work on natural fibers, and you generally need to finish or sew up your project before you do anything else. Projects are often blocked in pieces as well. Refer to specific instructions for your project to see what will work best.

Sometimes I have a knit sweater that needs just a little coaxing to shape it or make it lay flat. I spread it out on my ironing board and get the steam going on my iron. Without pressing the fabric directly with the iron, I steam the piece until the fabric is moistened. Then I move the fabric to the shape or flatness I am trying to achieve, and I leave it to dry. You may want to lay it flat on a towel on the floor or a large table to dry. You may need to pin the knitted fabric down to the flat surface to hold it in place while drying. That's basically the extent to which I block anything. To block or not to block, that is the question. The answer is if you need to change a little something, go ahead and block. If you like the size and look of your project, then leave it alone!

KITCHENER STITCH

Kitchener stitch is used to graft live stitches together. This means that the two sets of stitches are joined in a way that is continuous, without any seam.

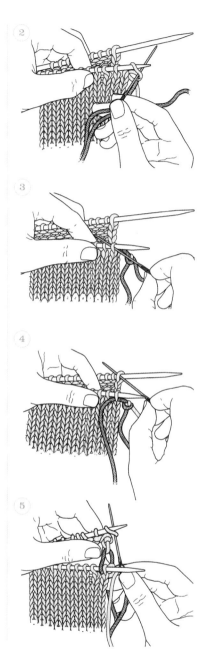

1. Place the stitches to be grafted so they are evenly divided on two needles with the points of the needles facing to the right, and the needles parallel so one needle is in front and the other is in back. The wrong sides of the fabric are facing each other.

2. With a length of matching yarn threaded into a yarn needle, insert the yarn needle through the first stitch on the front needle as if to knit and drop it off of the needle.

3. Then insert the yarn needle through the second stitch on the front needle as if to purl. Do not drop that stitch off of the needle; pull the yarn through.

4. On the back needle, insert the yarn needle through the first stitch as if to purl and drop it off of the needle.

5. Then insert the needle through the second stitch on the back needle as if to knit. Do not drop that stitch off of the needle; pull the yarn through.

* Repeat steps 2 through 5 until the stitches are all off of the needles. Weave in the end on the wrong side.

POM-POMS, TASSELS, AND FRINGE

POM-POMS

You will need cardboard strips cut to the width the pattern requires, scissors, and a yarn needle to attach the pom-poms. You can use different widths and wraps to create different looks.

Here, for example, is a pattern to make the 2-inch pom-pom with 40 wraps needed for the Baby Box Covers.

1. Cut a 2-inch strip of cardboard.

2. Wrap the yarn around the cardboard 40 times and cut the end.

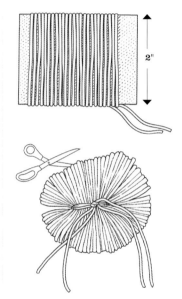

3. Tie an 8-inch length of yarn tightly around the center of the wrapped yarn using a double knot (tie the yarn as if you were beginning to tie your shoe, then do it again). The cardboard needs to be carefully pulled from the center before doing this, as you need to tie all the way around the wrapped yarn.

4. Slide your scissors into the loops and snip, making sure you cut through all of the loops.

5. Give the pom-pom a trim. You can clean up the shape by trimming the uneven ends.

Attach the pom-pom by threading the ends from the tie into a yarn needle and pulling the ends through to the wrong side of the knitted fabric. Secure the pom-pom with a few small stitches, then weave in the ends.

TIP • I have a great trick for tying a knot without the extra finger needed to keep it from slipping. Use a surgical knot. When you are making the double knot, bring the yarn under twice instead of just once and pull up tight. This extra time under keeps the knot from slipping before you make the second half of your knot.

TASSELS

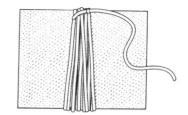

1. Cut a piece of cardboard to the width directed in the pattern.

2. Wrap the yarn the desired number of times around the cardboard.

3. Thread an 8-inch length of yarn into a yarn needle and slide it through the middle of the wrapped yarn. Tie with a double knot at the top of the wrapped yarn. Gently remove the wrapped yarn from the cardboard.

4. With another 8-inch length of yarn, wrap around all of the loops about a third of the way from the top of the tassel and tie using a double knot. You can wrap around the tie more than once for extra support on a larger tassel. Leave these ends long for now.

5. Slide your scissors in the loops and snip. Trim all uneven ends. Take the loose ends from the tie, pull them under the wrapped yarn, and pull them through to the center of the tassel. Trim these to match the rest of the tassel.

6. Attach the tassel by running the ends left at the top of the tassel through to the wrong side of the knitted fabric. Tie the ends and weave them in.

FRINGE

1. Cut the yarn to the length and the number of pieces desired.

2. Holding 2 strands of yarn (or the desired number) together, fold them in half.

3. Lay the knitted fabric on a table in front of you. Insert a crochet hook through the fabric from back to front and under 2 loops of the stitch on the edge. This will provide more support for the fringe.

4. Insert the crochet hook into the loop end of the folded strands and pull the strands halfway through the stitch.

5. Pull the cut ends through their own loops with the crochet hook. Tighten the fringe by gently pulling the cut ends. Trim if necessary.

CROCHET TECHNIQUES

SLIP KNOT

The slip knot is the very first step to begin crochet.

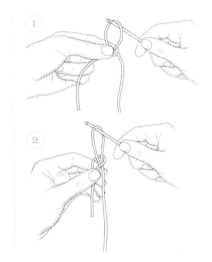

1. Measure out about 4 inches from the tail end of the ball of yarn. You will make a slip knot at this point on the yarn.

2. Make a loop, overlapping the yarn at the bottom of the loop.

3. Bring the yarn that is on top of the overlap behind and then through the loop, making another loop. Pull up.

4. Put the new loop on the hook and tighten it to fit.

CHAIN STITCH

The chain stitch is the place to start when learning to crochet. With a slip knot on the hook, with the hook in your right hand, and with your left hand holding the working yarn as you would for continental knitting, continue as follows:

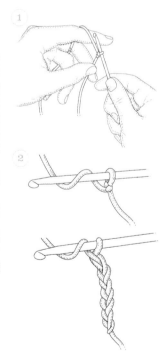

1. Wrap the yarn over the hook from back to front (counterclockwise).

2. Catching the yarn with your hook, pull it through the loop on the hook. (You may need to hold the slip knot with the thumb and middle finger of your left hand to keep it steady.)

• Repeat steps 1 and 2 until desired number of chain stitches are made.

SLIP STITCH

The slip stitch is often used to join rounds when crocheting in a circle or when making a picot edging.

1. Insert the hook into the two upper strands of the appropriate stitch as directed in the pattern.

2. Wrap the yarn over the hook from back to front (counterclockwise) and pull it through the stitch.

3. With two loops on the hook, pull the second loop through the first loop.

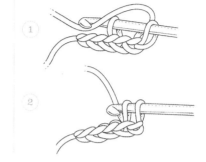

SINGLE CROCHET

The single crochet is one of the first stitches you'll need to learn. It is the most basic stitch, but it can be used to create almost anything.

1. Insert the hook into the two upper strands of the appropriate stitch as directed in the pattern.

2. Wrap the yarn over the hook from back to front (counterclockwise) and pull it through the stitch.

3. Wrap the yarn over the hook once more and pull it through both loops.

• Repeat as directed.

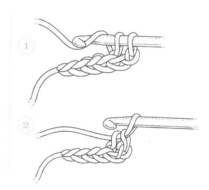

EMBROIDERY TECHNIQUES

SPIDER WEB

This embroidery technique is one of my favorites for making dots on knitted fabric. It is simple, quick, and fun.

1. Begin by making 5 straight stitches radiating out from a center point. These stitches form spokes and are the foundation for the spider web.

2. Next, stitching up from the center, begin weaving the needle over and under the spokes until they are completely covered.

3. Pull the yarn through to the wrong side of the fabric and secure by taking a few small stitches. Trim the end close to the fabric.

5 straight stitches.

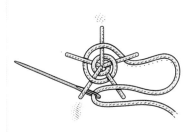

Stitch end over and under the spokes until the straight stitches are covered.

BACKSTITCH

The backstitch is used to make lines that are straight or curved. Make the stitches small and as even as possible.

1. Cut a length of yarn and thread it into a yarn needle. Pull the yarn through several loops on the wrong side of the fabric, leaving a ½-inch tail. With the needle, pull the yarn through to the right side at your starting point.

2. Moving backward from your starting point, insert your needle at 2 and have the point of the needle come out at 3. This should be one motion.

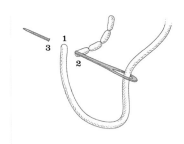

3. Pull the yarn through, insert the needle into the new 2, and have the point of the needle come out at 3.

- Keep working in this way, moving backward and forward, until you have completed the length of stitching desired. At the last stitch, pull the yarn through to the back and weave in the end on the wrong side of the knitted fabric.

SATIN STITCH

The satin stitch is used to fill in spaces and to create a certain shape. It is worked in one motion and moves quickly.

1. Cut a length of yarn and thread it into a yarn needle. Pull the yarn through several loops on the wrong side of the fabric. Pull the needle through to the right side, at the starting point.

2. Insert the needle at 2 and have the point of the needle come out at 3. Pull the yarn through.

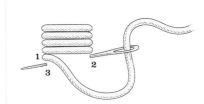

- Repeat step 2 until the space is filled. On the last stitch, pull the yarn through to the wrong side of the knitted fabric and weave in the end.

RUNNING STITCH

1. Cut a length of yarn and thread it into a yarn needle. Pull the yarn through several loops on the wrong side of the fabric. Pull the yarn through to the right side. This is your starting point.

2. Insert the needle at 2 and bring it up at 3, pulling the yarn through in one motion.

3. Insert the needle at 4 and bring it up at 5, pulling the yarn through in one motion.

- Repeat to the end for the desired length. Pull the yarn through to the wrong side of the knitted fabric. Weave in the end.

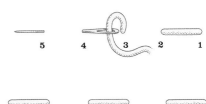

STRAIGHT STITCH

1. Cut a length of yarn and thread it into a yarn needle. Pull the yarn through several loops on the wrong side of the fabric. Pull the needle through to the open middle of the knitted hole. This is the starting point.

2. Insert the needle at 2 and bring the needle back through the open middle. Pull the yarn through.

3. Insert the needle at 3 and bring the needle back through the open middle. Pull the yarn through.

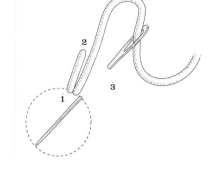

• Continue in this way until you have filled in the border of the hole. You may have to overlap the stitches somewhat to get a solid look. Don't worry if all of the stitches are not the exact same length (mine aren't and probably never will be); this adds more character.

CHAIN STITCH THROUGH KNITTED FABRIC

This stitch looks like the embroidered lazy daisy stitch. I don't worry about having perfect uniformity of my stitches mainly because I use this as a foundation line to complete a wrapping technique or a weaving technique, both of which cover the chain stitch lines. Here is how I crochet a chain stitch directly onto my knitted fabric:

1. Holding the working yarn to the back of the knitted fabric, insert your crochet hook into the intended starting point from the right side of the fabric and push through to the wrong side of the fabric.

2. Make a loop around the hook with the working yarn, and pull the loop through the fabric to the right side. You now have one loop on the crochet hook.

3. Insert the hook back through the fabric to the wrong side, moving along the fabric in the intended direction. Make a loop around the hook with the working yarn, and pull the loop through the fabric to the right side. Pull this loop through the first loop on the hook. You have one loop remaining on the hook.

4. Repeat steps 2 and 3, forming the intended shape or line as you complete the stitches.

5. On the last stitch, cut the yarn and pull the end through to the right side. Thread the end into a yarn needle, and pull the end through to the wrong side of the fabric. Secure the last chain stitch in place with a small stitch. Weave in the end.

WRAPPING STITCH

This is my variation on both the overcast stitch and a couching embroidery technique, but it is slightly different because it isn't exactly like either of these stitches of old. I use this technique wherever I get a chance because I love the textured, wormy appearance it gives the knitted fabric. The wrapping stitch is used on the Stroller Blanket, the Chubby Bunny, Frenchie, and the *Bébé* Hanging Sachet. Warning, this is addictve!

1. Using the chain stitch through the knitted fabric (see p. 154) as the foundation for the shape or line you intend to wrap, thread a 12- to 18-inch piece of yarn into a yarn needle. Secure the yarn on the wrong side of the fabric by taking a couple of small stitches through the chain stitches. Bring the needle and the yarn to the right side of the fabric, at the starting point.

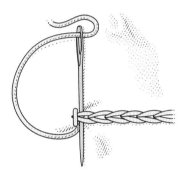

Steps 1 and 2

2. Next make tiny satin stitches around the chain stitches, very close together and working only on the right side of the fabric. Make these stitches tight and close together so that you don't see the chain stitch foundation.

3. After the last stitch is completed, pull the yarn through to the wrong side of the fabric, and make a couple of tiny stitches through the chain stitches to secure the end and cut the end close to the fabric.

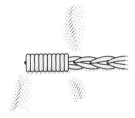

Step 3

WOVEN DOTS

I wanted to create a new textured polka dot to embellish my knitted fabric. I love the idea of weaving yarn to create circles. These turned out great, and I used them on the Baby Box Covers. You could use them to create polka dots on any knitted project!

1. Begin by working a circle with a crochet hook and the chain stitch through the knitted fabric (see p. 158). I always make these circles freehand and don't worry if they are perfectly round. Imperfection only adds more interest.

2. With a length of yarn about 12 to 18 inches long threaded into a yarn needle, begin making satin stitches across the circle from the left side of the circle to the right side of the circle until the circle is covered.

3. Continuing on with the same length of yarn, begin weaving the yarn needle over and under the satin stitches from the top of the circle to the bottom of the circle to create a woven surface. Repeat step 3 until the circle is completely covered.

4. Pull the end through to the wrong side of the fabric and weave in by taking a few small stitches. Trim neatly.

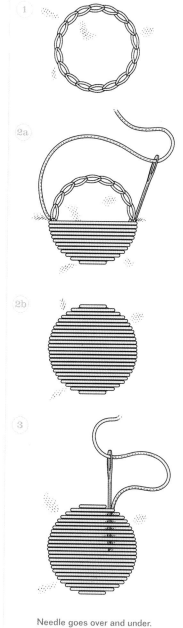

Needle goes over and under.

SPLIT STITCH

The split stitch is great for making lines on the surface of the knitted fabric. Usually in knitting you don't want to split the yarn, but in this embroidery stitch that is exactly what you are doing. I used the split stitch on the Cozy Book Pillow and Sweater to embroider little stars for added detail. Here's what you do:

1. Begin by making a small straight stitch.

2. When you come up for the next stitch, come through the middle of the yarn of the first straight stitch, splitting the stitch, and pull the yarn through. Make another stitch in the intended direction and pull through to the wrong side of the fabric. Repeat, splitting the yarn each time you take a stitch.

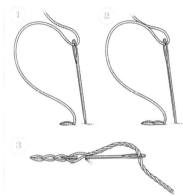

FRENCH KNOTS

I used French knots combined with the split stitch on the Cozy Book-Pillow set to create stars. It's a great decorative stitch. However, my French knots, even when done exactly according to others' instructions, never turn out quite right. So here is my own twist on this technique.

1. Cut a length of yarn and thread it into a yarn needle. Pull the yarn through several loops on the wrong side of the fabric. Pull the yarn through to the right side of the fabric. This will place the French knot.

2. Wrap the yarn around the needle three times while holding the needle close to the fabric. Hold the yarn wraps taut by pinching the yarn between your left thumb and index finger. Insert the needle nearby and pull it gently through to wrong side of the fabric.

3. Insert the needle right next to the wraps and pull the yarn through to the right side of the fabric.

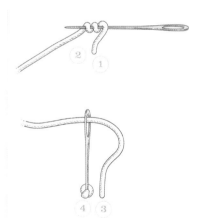

4. Insert the needle into the center of the knot just created and pull it through to the wrong side of the fabric. This extra stitch makes the French knot much more secure and gives it a finished look.

· If you are making one knot, cut the yarn and weave in the end. If you are making many knots, carry the yarn over the back of your work to different spots, but only if you can't see the carried yarn through the fabric. If you can see it from the right side, you'll have to cut your yarn and tie it off for each French knot, then reattach the yarn at the new spots as you go.

sources

Blue Sky Alpacas, Inc.
P.O. Box 88
Cedar, MN 55011
888-460-8862
www.blueskyalpacas.com

Can o' Clips
(mini clothespins)
Cavallini & Co.
401 Forbes Boulevard
South San Francisco, CA 94808
650-616-4500
www.cavallini.com

Cascade Yarns
1224 Andover Park East
Tukwila, WA 98188
206-574-0440
www.cascadeyarns.com

Crystal Palace Yarns
160 23rd Street
Richmond, CA 94804
510-237-9988
www.straw.com

Fleurishes (ribbon)
2848 University Avenue
Madison, WI 53705
608-238-5555
www.fleurishes.com

The Garment District
(feather boas)
200 Broadway
Cambridge, MA 02139
617-876-1122
www.garmentdistrict.com

GGH
Distributed by Muench Yarns
1323 Scott Street
Petaluma, CA 94954
800-733-9276
www.muenchyarns.com

Manos del Uruguay
Distributed by Design Source
P.O. Box 770
Medford, MA 02180
888-566-9970
www.manos.com.uy

Noro
Distributed by Knitting Fever
P.O. Box 336
315 Bayview Avenue
Amityville, NY 11701
516-546-3000
www.knittingfever.com

Rowan and RYC
Distributed by Westminster
Fibers
4 Townsend West, Unit 8
Nashua, NH 03063
800-445-9276
www.knitrowan.com
www.ryclassic.com

USA Baby (mobiles)
793 Springer Drive
Lombard, IL 60148
800-323-4108
www.usababy.com

INTERNET-ONLY SOURCES

www.shopabcsoup.com
My own Web site is a place to
purchase knitting kits for this
book, as well as other baby
goodies.

www.susanbanderson
.blogspot.com
My blog is the place to go for
updates on *Itty-Bitty Nursery* and
other events.

These four places are all great
sources for yarn.

www.patternworks.com

www.jimmybearswool.com

www.purlsoho.com

www.yarnmarket.com

www.tinyzippers.com
For small zippers.

acknowledgments

The stars must have been aligned the day I first contacted Artisan about writing a book. For me it has been a match made in heaven. My publisher, Ann Bramson, has been a constant source of guidance and support. Ann, as always, thank you for giving me the most wonderful opportunities any author could hope for. My books are a personal, heartfelt expression of my love for knitting, and you let that shine through. Your talent is inspiring.

Thank you to all of the people who spent too many hours to count working on *Itty-Bitty Nursery*. I'd like to send out a huge thank you to Trent Duffy for his top-notch editing talents and sense of humor, Jan Derevjanik and Stephanie Huntwork for their fantastic book design skills, and Jaime Harder and Danielle Costa for being ever supportive. These are just a few of the Artisan staff on whom I depend. You make my job much easier, and I appreciate you all at Artisan. A special thanks to my copy editor, Andrea Molitor, for her excellent editing skills and her knitting expertise.

Liz Banfield, who once again came through with her photography genius to make this book a baby spectacular. You are a great talent, Liz, and I love working with you. Your work makes the book come alive. Thank you for your dedication, through thick and thin, and through one more pregnancy! And I would like to give a big hug to the adorable models she lined up: Hadley and Cathryn Williams, Foster and Nicole Gerlac, Janelle and Kaylee Streich, Tripp Beltz, Shepherd Sorenson, Piper Lee, Reece Woollen, Pearl Awad, Truth Mabon, Chloe Bispala, Nora Lescarbeau, Mia Collins, Witt Mehbod, and, of course, Grier McPherson (Liz's son). Thanks to their parents as well!

To my sweet family, you are my world. I love and appreciate you all, Brian, Evan, Ben, Holly, and Mary Kate. Brian, thanks for giving me the gift of time, which is no small feat in our hectic life. I appreciate all of the sacrifices you have made in order for this book to happen. Thank you.

To my dear mother, Mary Ann Barrett, thank you for your unconditional support and love, and for sewing the lining and zipper in the stroller jacket. Beautifully done! Thanks for helping with the kids, and for being the most fantastic mother and grandmother ever. I hope someday to be just like you.

Thanks to Jim Mueller for my author photograph and to Laura Mueller for the constant support and friendship.

Thanks to all of the knitters who inspire me to keep knitting and designing. Your enthusiasm is contagious!

ABOUT THE AUTHOR

Susan B. Anderson began her knitting career at the age of nineteen with an instruction booklet, some needles, and yarn. Today she sells her one-of-a-kind pieces under her 4 Busy Kids Knitting Studio label, as well as through her online knitted boutique, www.shopabcsoup.com. Her knitting blog (http://susanbanderson.blogspot.com) has a coterie of devoted readers. The author of *Itty-Bitty Hats* (Artisan, 2006), she lives in Madison, Wisconsin, with her husband and four children.